LETTERS
FROM TULLY

Estella Bowen Culp—"Tully" (family photo)

LETTERS FROM TULLY

A Woman's Life on the Dakota Frontier

Estella Bowen Culp

Johnson Books
BOULDER

Published by Johnson Books, a Big Earth Publishing company,
3005 Center Green Drive, Suite 220, Boulder, Colorado 80301.
E-mail: books@bigearthpublishing.com
www.bigearthpublishing.com
1-800-258-5830

Cover and text design by Constance Bollen, cbgraphics
Permission was kindly given by Elsie Hey Baye to use photos from her book
Haaken Horizons.

9   8   7   6   5   4   3   2   1

Library of Congress Cataloging-in-Publication Data
Culp, Estella Bowen.
 [Correspondence. Selections]
 Letters from Tully: a woman's life on the Dakota frontier / by Estella Bowen Culp.
   p. cm.
 ISBN 1-55566-403-2
 1. Culp, Estella Bowen. [1. Frontier and pioneer life—South Dakota. 2. Women—
South Dakota—Biography.] I. Title.
 CT275.C9278A4 2006
 978.3'01092—dc22
 [B]
                              2006036509

Printed in the United States of America

Contents

The manuscript for Letters from Tully, *written by my Great Aunt Estella (who was frequently called Stell by her family) and begun in 1906, floated for decades after her death from one relative to another to read. Each time it was passed around, it was said over and over, "We should get this published." When it came to me several months ago, and I read it again, I too, said, "This should be published." I called Mira Perrizo, publisher of Johnson Books. She read the manuscript, and after consulting with her colleagues, agreed with me. I sought the consent of other surviving cousins, who also agreed to publication. We hope that you will enjoy reading the letters about the seventeen years of Estella Bowen Culp's unique life as a homesteader in Philip, South Dakota.*

—S. Sue McMillan

Foreword

This collection of letters by schoolteacher Estella Culp, written between 1906 and 1923, gives us rare insight into events surrounding the final phase of settlement on the South Dakota frontier. In part sparked by railway companies that saw future profits in developing the last open patches of land west of the Missouri River, the federal government opened the Cheyenne Reservation for agricultural development by both Native American and white settlers. In 1906 newlyweds Estella and Orley Culp signed up for 160 acres near Philip, South Dakota, south of the Cheyenne River, in order to fulfill their dream of home ownership. The final patent, or deed, to Estella Culp's property is dated March 16, 1908.

Pioneers at this time little resembled earlier settlers who arrived only by covered wagon or mule train. Now they poured into the West by train. Estella herself enjoyed a break from the long ride on a covered wagon from Wakefield, Nebraska, when she traveled on the newly built rail line between Presho and Murdo.

Although many parts of the country could then be reached by rail, the conditions under which civic life evolved were nevertheless primitive and adventurous. Consequently, many settlers remained only long enough on their homestead to "prove up," or satisfy the minimum requirement for permanent ownership, and then sell out for a profit.

Estella (far left) with her mother and father
and seven siblings. (family photo)

As a young girl, Estella's immediate family had settled on homesteads in Kansas, but instead of farming she was sent to live with an aunt and uncle who encouraged an intellectual career as schoolteacher. With no experience in farming or animal husbandry, Estella was unprepared for the hardships that would face her in South Dakota. Despite many setbacks, she and Orley would stay on their newly acquired land for nineteen years. She writes: "It does not seem that an intelligent woman capable of making a good living anywhere would be willing to go through with all these experiences just for a humble little place that we can call our own home." Also typical, many of these latter day settlers did not come alone but brought other family members who settled on neighboring parcels of land. Estella's mother, Lucy A. Bowen, who became an experienced homesteader in Kansas when she was just a young married woman, filed for land in Haakon County as did Estella's sister Mabel A. Bowen along with her husband. Having family nearby helped many overcome the loneliness of the prairie, Estella being no exception.

Estella's account is an insider's view into the typical hardships of life on the homestead, but its style and content reflect the spiritual journey of a woman who turned her experience on the frontier into a reflection on life in general. The narrative is based on a collection of letters addressed to one of her cousins in Kansas. Formally, the chapters resemble these individual letters, but they were probably edited by Estella herself years later to take on the form of an autobiography. The clue here is that she signs a "note" at the beginning of the Preface with E.B.T., which are the initials of her name after her next marriage. The chapters are carefully structured so that the ending of one chapter often anticipates the sentiment and events in the following section, thus making it a delightful read.

We don't know to what extent she intended to publish this memoir and what readership outside of her immediate family she wanted to address. Any historian might find it frustrating to use these writings to confirm the existence of particular citizens from the early days in Haakon County. She systematically alters names of family members and those of friends. She writes the letters to her

Ten-year-old Carrie N. Bowen and
eight-year-old Estella Annette Bowen. (family photo)

cousin Sara, who is actually her sister Carrie; sister Mabel in real life is her sister Anne in the book; and her brother Walt is Sam in the story. She even calls herself Tully, and her husband, Orley, becomes John. The events themselves are truthfully recounted and confirm official historical records from that time.

By the time Estella writes her letters home, time has erased memories of the pain and hardships involved and she employs a more nostalgic style. Her deft use of humor to relate hardship makes it easy for the careless reader to misunderstand the true ramifications of the many mistakes she and her husband make, leading her to remind the reader that "the past usually is pleasant to contemplate for the hardships resolve themselves into adventures as time moves on." With amusement she relates their misfortunes as clumsy homesteaders and farmers. When her husband accidentally plants alfalfa seedlings upside down she turns it into an entertaining anecdote. In retrospect, Estella's mature voice reflects the adventures of an inexperienced young woman on her homestead, who does not pass judgment on her unskilled handling of potential life threatening incidents. In an unheroic manner she tells how she deals with blizzards and dying livestock. Her unsentimental style invites the reader to evaluate and draw his or her own conclusions.

Nevertheless, she also reports on her many tears when the chain of misfortunes would not end. Those moments are especially well reflected in the numerous poems that one finds throughout the text: "Does God forget his nestlings / In such a plight as this? / Do they trust Him in times like these? / Who knows?"

East of the Missouri, along the banks of the Bad River where large buffalo herds once attracted diverse tribes of Native Americans and later fur traders to Fort Pierre, the land was rugged and the climate not well suited for farming. Without doubt, the reader will ask how anyone could endure under those conditions. Like a skilled novelist, Estella keeps the text suspenseful and the reader wonders until the very end if the hardships on the homestead will eventually be overcome.

At the time of Estella's arrival, the railway was not yet completed into Philip and land parcels wouldn't be issued until it was. The town was an accumulation of temporary shacks with makeshift law and order and remained in relative isolation until May 1907 when the Chicago and Northwestern Railroad finally reached the site. By then the railway company was willing to sell individual lots and Philip could finally emerge as a rightful town. In Estella's view, since the town did not formally exist upon her arrival, it did not merit much literary attention and so the first part of this memoir focuses on her experiences on the homestead and chronicles the hardships brought about by natural rather than manmade forces.

Estella's homestead was located on what was known during the nineteenth century as the Great American Desert, now more accurately named the Great Plains, which describes the area west of the Mississippi River. Before the arrival of fur traders and large cattle companies during the mid- to late nineteenth century, the area was mainly inhabited by tribes of Native Americans. For a long time, Americans considered the land to be unfit for habitation. After President Benjamin Harrison officially opened the Grand Sioux Reservation of South Dakota to homesteaders in 1892, Native American tribes were sequestered on smaller portions of land on

*This early picture of Philip shows the orderly development that
followed after the town lot sale. Center Avenue is taking shape and
famous Railroad Street boasts business firms also. In the background
is the Chicago Northwestern Railroad, which arrived in the first year
of the town to bring contact with the outside world as well as
supplying the new city and surrounding territory.*
(First Half Century, Philip, South Dakota)

the Rosebud Reservation south of Philip, and the Cheyenne
Reservation north of the Cheyenne and White Rivers. Settlers now
were able to farm in those regions, and by the time Estella arrived,
major disputes between settlers and Native Americans were largely
resolved. The chapter that she devotes to her Native American
neighbors might initially have been an attempt to portray the proud
native of the Great Plains, fierce and a potential threat to lonely
white women on the homestead. But ultimately it renders a sad
picture of a passive and subdued group of indigenous peoples. We

learn about tribes that have been divided territorially and of those who have fallen victim to alcohol.

The land around Philip is dry and desertlike. And yet, the combined Missouri-Mississippi River system is the fourth-longest river in the world. It covers more than 2,500 miles from northern Minnesota to the Gulf of Mexico. It has 250 tributaries and its flood plain covers 1.25 million square miles. Consequently, in times of heavy rainfall, this dry land is subject to soaring and devastating floods. Estella describes one of the floods along the Bad River in 1910 as being as unusual as a flood would be in the Sahara Desert. Because of the lack of trees on large portions of the Great Plains, it tends to be windy all year round. In winter the weather is very cold with the wind blowing snow into blizzards. The summers are very hot and windy, which dries and cracks the land, making farming a challenge. Yet, in Estella's words, spring can turn this unforgiving land into a delightful experience:

> *When South Dakota smiles, she smiles. The weather in the spring and fall is very pleasant. The air has such a delightful tang. It makes you want to work. The days are balmy and warm and the stars at night seem near enough so that you can almost pick them from the sky.*

These are not the words of a farmer, but of a poet who uses the landscape metaphorically as a source of strength and hope that will eventually let her overcome the unforgiving forces of nature. When the prairie is covered with an abundance of flowers and wildlife, Estella adds that "the prospect of all this wild fruit made me more

September 22, 1909, the bustling town had its third fire.
The building that burned was three doors up from the 73 saloon.
(Photo courtesy Mrs. Max Husband,
First Half Century, Philip, South Dakota*)*

hopeful of making a living here. If we can do so, I am sure that I shall never want to live anywhere else."

When flood waters abated, prairie fires were another threat to the lives of many. Estella speaks of fires on the prairies as one of the most feared events for the homesteaders. In the fall of 1907 Estella witnesses a fire in the town of Philip that was nourished by strong prairie winds. Many structures were consumed by the flames and the "terror on the faces" of the victims "transformed them until you could scarcely recognize them." Her own house in the town was destroyed by fire in 1909. This wasn't the last time that she herself fell victim to flames.

Her house on the homestead remains primitive to the end. She and Orley depend on other jobs to earn money with which they hope to eventually build the foundation of a sustainable farm. From season to season they move between their homestead and accommodations in Philip. In 1909 she laments that "we haven't had a home since we came into town; we have simply had a place to stay." In the end, her teacher's income makes ends meet.

In its issue of April 4, 1907, the *Bad River News* reported that the "Philip school opened Monday with an enrollment of 21 pupils and Mrs. Culp as teacher." Although the primitive conditions of the log school resemble the crude state of the homestead, she greatly anticipates the moment of finally again working in her beloved profession as teacher. Surprisingly, Estella shows little concern when she first visits the primitive log school house where she would leave her first mark in the historical records of Philip. The school is full of dust and dirt, it attracts mice and rattlesnakes, and the space is inadequate for the ever growing number of children of new homesteaders that were to attend her classes.

In 1948, shortly before her death, Estella remembers her first teaching position:

I came to a homestead five miles west of Philip in August, 1906. The next spring I taught in the log schoolhouse. A barrelshape stove stood in the center of the room. The teacher's desk was an ordinary kitchen table. There was a blackboard across the front of the room. A heavy door hung on one hinge at the entrance, and when all the children were in their place the door could not be opened. To open the door it was necessary to move some of the rude benches, and for

the children who used them to stand near the middle of the room.
There was one outhouse and that was used by both boys and girls.
And it had a gunny sack door. (Haakon Horizons, *p. 203*)

The *Bad River News* also reports of a school meeting where "the county superintendent spoke, and papers were read by Mrs. Culp." If farming proved to be a seemingly insurmountable challenge, teaching gained Estella the trust of the community to which she accredits her willpower to perservere. While Orley worked odd jobs at the railroad, in restaurants, and the local hotel to supplement the farm income, Estella's teaching position presented the most stable source of income for the couple and provided, above all, an escape from loneliness on the farm. Her landscape descriptions provide a barometer of her feelings toward her life as a homesteader versus her life as a professional teacher; the former are lonely and fearful, the latter bright and happy. As an educator her local fame increased. Historical records report that in 1908, when the little log schoolhouse became too small to accommodate the number of frontier children, the school board transferred Estella and her pupils to a two-room frame structure. Estella describes the relocation when, once again, great improvisation skills were required:

School opened late in October in an unfinished building which had
neither doors nor windows put yet in place. There was no school
furniture of any kind.We put planks around the rooms on nail kegs,
and at first some of the children sat on the floor and used the planks
for desks. After a few days, the children sat on the planks or rude

benches at such tables as we were able to provide. The situation lasted about a month. (Haakon Horizons, *p. 205*)

Estella's activities in the educational community of Philip helped her avoid the isolation many homesteaders experienced, particularly women, whose work was often restricted to domestic tasks with little connection to the outside world. Her letters often recount the loneliness out on the prairie and the fear of being exposed and vulnerable to unknown dangers, natural or human by nature. Those fears bred the kind of homesickness that for many meant the beginning of the end of homesteading altogether. Here, Estella provides the reader a glimpse into the gender-specific challenges that await the settlers:

There is something about the life in the vast expanse of the prairies which seems to appeal to man. The spirit of adventure is so firmly planted in them that they like a contest of any kind. The contest for life in this new, untried country satisfies this love of adventure to some extent. They get a thrill out of the living. . . . With women it is quite a different proposition. When you meet a woman who has the heart hunger in her eyes, you know that the homesickness has begun and sooner or later that family would be leaving this country. Often the wife goes "back home" to visit her family. Sometimes she comes back satisfied to stay a while longer, but when she has once had a case of real homesickness, the new country has lost its appeal and she is no longer willing to live in this primitive fashion, and the family returns to the old home, or else they go where they can have the comforts this civilization affords.

As Estella enjoys her newly acquired position as teacher and school headmaster in Philip, the latter part of her memoir focuses more on the importance of the community and the valuable support that friends provided during the hardships of all these years. When she gets on the train that will carry her even further west to a new and better career opportunity in Wyoming, she concludes with a note on her friends: "Leaving this group of faithful friends was one of the hardest things that I had ever been called upon to do."

The reader realizes now what might have been the account of an unsuccessful homesteading experience turns into an evaluation of spiritual values. We no longer hear the voice of a woman who had lamented earlier that she couldn't live up to the standards set by her pioneer mother and grandmother: "My grandmother was a pioneer, my mother was a pioneer and I was not going to be any less brave than they had been." In early chapters she is torn between her role as young wife and devotion to the farmland, between her commitment to turning a profit on the land and her desire to turn the wilderness into a private garden. Endless demands and repetitive failures almost lead to a devaluation of herself and her abilities: fear, self-doubt, and guilt. She feels entrapped in the vastness of the land, exposed to the elements that could crush her any moment. The openness of the country becomes a prison. In writing, she reclaims control over her destiny, once lost to her failures.

In the end, Estella reexamines success in a different framework, where the writing process itself is a tool that helps her to come to terms with the world. In the final chapter in particular, while Estella succumbs to the failure of homesteading, she achieves a greater sense of spiritual self. The work reveals more than the physical struggle; it unveils something of the author's psychological journey. If the letters were originally meant to sketch life in the new country, Estella now turned them into a tool of self-examination. Her decision to leave Philip for Wyoming is met with the following lines: "During this talk with John [Orley] the feeling of loss and failure seemed to leave me and I realized for the first time in years that we had not lost. While our venture in farming had not brought financial returns, it had brought spiritual values which only come to people who live through hardships without becoming embittered."

She speaks for all those whose life seemed not to follow the success story of the American Dream but who nevertheless left a crucial milestone for others to set their sights on. Her concluding words are those of a teacher who sees a promising future in the eyes of a young student: "It was time for us to move on and let the younger generation start where we had left off." She speaks for so many whose voices were drowned and whose dreams were shattered in the cruel vastness of the frontier. Their untold struggles can now be celebrated through Estella's letters back home.

Anja K. Lange, Ph.D.
University of Colorado
Herbst Program of Humanities

LETTERS
FROM TULLY

Preface

Note: *The experiences related in this book are my own. I have given myself the name of Tully Graves in the story. All the characters in the story have been given fictitious names.*

Signed E.B.T. (Estella Bowen Culp Tener)

This book contains some of the pioneer experiences of Tully Graves, a woman who gave up a position in the high school in Wakefield, Nebraska, to go with her husband, John Graves, into western South Dakota where they took up a homestead and endeavored to establish a home.

Although she was the child of a pioneer, she had spent the greater part of her life, previous to her marriage, in the home of an Aunt and Uncle who were in comfortable circumstances. Being the only child in this home, she had been so shielded that she had never even spent an evening alone, until she was married about three years before. Many times the thought of going out on the lonely prairie filled her with terror, yet each time the longing for a home of her own and a strong desire to give John a chance to make good overruled her fears, and made her determined to do her part toward making the homestead venture a success.

John Graves was a struggling man-of-all work in the little Nebraska town where they lived. He was unable to make his adjust-

Tully / Estella (family photo)

ment in the community so that it seemed impossible for him to hold a job that enabled him to keep up a home.

It was in the spring of the year 1906 when he heard that the government was opening up a part of the Sioux Indian reservation in South Dakota for settlement. In March he made a trip up into that country and filed on one hundred and sixty acres of land between the North and South Forks of Bad River about ninety miles west of Pierre and about seventy miles northwest of Murdo. He returned home and began to make plans for going back there to live, for in six months after making this filing it was necessary for him to take up his residence upon the land and begin to make his improvements. After eight months of actual residence upon the land, he could prove up for fifty cents an acre.

There was a railroad being built into this newly opened tract, but it was not completed farther than Pierre. As this made it necessary for the Graves to drive a part of the way at least, they decided to make the trip all the way in a covered wagon.

John bought a new wagon and put it in the back yard where he worked on it mornings and evenings, fitting it up so that it would make a home for the family during the trip and also until the new home was finished on the claim in South Dakota.

There were no sentimental treasures to be put in the wagon. All of these were to be stored and shipped later when the railroad was finished.

Only the bed and necessary cooking utensils, clothing and tools together with a crate of chickens fastened on to the

Sister Mabel, who is Anne in the book. (family photo)

back of the wagon made up the load when all was finished in early August.

The Graves had bought a team of three year old bay mare colts. They were handsome and gentle, but not well broken.

John Graves had not done much farming, but he was eager for the adventure as was also his wife, Tully, and his sister-in-law, Anne, who were going to make the trip through with them in the covered wagon. They planned to start soon after noon on the ninth day of August but those colts kept them all three busy until late afternoon trying to get them hitched to the wagon.

When Mrs. Graves was bidding her relatives good bye, her cousin Sara said, "Tully, please write and tell me all about your trip, how you build your new home, and much details about your life in that new country"; hence the following letters were written a little at a time at irregular intervals and not sent until they were huge and bulky.

———————

Note: *Photos were added for the enjoyment of the reader, but they were not part of Tully's original letters. The letters have been reprinted as written and retain Tully's original voice and spelling.*

Our Trip

My dear Sara:

Here we are at last on the homestead. I am seated on the bed in our only house, the covered wagon, writing to you by the light of the lantern.

I just learned that I could send some mail down to the post office tomorrow by a neighbor who is going in to bring groceries for all of us. We came through Philip day before yesterday, and I bought food enough to last us for a week, I thought, but we are so hungry here that we have eaten it all up so soon.

John has gone back with the team and wagon to Anne's place for the rest of our lumber. I think that it will take him at least two days for the trip for it is twenty-two miles over there. The return trip with the load of lumber will be very slow. That leaves us with no way of getting about. When this neighbor drove by yesterday and asked if he could bring out some groceries for us tomorrow, I told him that his neighborly act would save our family from starvation for a ten mile walk to the store and back seemed out of the question to me.

We got your letters when we came through Philip day before yesterday and were not at all surprised that you people were worried about us, for we had not written to you for so long. You will understand how it all came about when I tell you some of the things that have happened on the trip.

To begin with our wagon was overloaded. Those two handsome bay mare colts were beautiful to look at, but they were too young and too soft for the ordeal that was before them. The struggle we had in hitching them up that afternoon we left made us so very late starting that we were unable to make more than nine miles that first afternoon. We camped for the night near the Logan River not far from a farm house.

In the middle of the night some rowdies rode up on horse back to give us a scare I guess. They began to shout to us and rode their horses so close that their noses brushed against the canvas of the wagon cover. John shouted, "Get the ————- out of here or I'll drill you," and reached for his shot gun which hung within his easy reach, made fast to the side of the wagon by straps which held it in place. As he drew back the flap from the front of the wagon, he saw the riders disappearing down the road at full gallop. They seemed to sense that he was not a man who cared to be disturbed in his home even if that home was only a covered wagon.

"Poor me," I was simply frozen with fear at first. I could not move and then I shook until my teeth chattered. John and sister Anne told me not to be so silly but to go on back to sleep. Sleep was not for me that night. I wished myself safely out of it all. Over and over again I kept saying what ever could have induced us to think that we could make this three hundred mile trip in a covered wagon and why did we want to go out on a homestead anyway when we knew so little about horses or anything connected with a farm. I don't know why I chose the wee hours of the night to think this thing through as John and I had gone over it again and again since we decided to take up a homestead. Then I would think of one hundred and sixty acres of land for fifty cents an acre. Suppose it was a part of the Sioux Indian reservation. My grandmother was a pioneer, my mother was a pioneer and I was not going to be any less brave than they had been. I hate lying awake at nights moralizing to myself and I was very glad when I drew back the flap of the canvas and saw that dawn was approaching. As I lay there looking out into the darkness a grey light crept over everything changing the dark shadows that had looked like black clouds, hugging the ground along the river banks, into trees that stood out more and more vividly as the sunlight now touched their tops and brought out the rich green color of the leaves.

I now became conscious that the air was filled with the fragrance of growing things. I wanted to get up right away so that I could see all about me and enjoy this early morning in the country.

I call John and sister Anne and we were soon bustling about cooking our bacon, eggs and coffee over a camp fire. This was my first experience at cooking breakfast over a camp fire. John had built such a big fire that I soon felt I would be cooked before the bacon was and I called for help. John brought a long forked stick to handle the skillet and coffee pot with. He soon had plenty of bacon and eggs ready. Bacon is good at any time, but I never tasted such delicious bacon as we had at morning. Those long, crispy brown strips fairly melted in your mouth and since there is no coffee quite so good as camp coffee, I felt that this breakfast compensated in a measure for my sleepless night.

Our new big job was to get those colts hitched to that wagon again. It proved to be a real job. The colts were afraid and so were we. They did not know what to do, and neither did we. It was almost ten o'clock before we got on our way. We stopped about one o'clock for our lunch and to rest the horses. While we were packing up and getting ready to move on, we noticed a heavy black cloud coming up in the northwest, but we thought it was moving to the south and that if we hurried we could keep out of the path of the storm, accordingly we urged those pretty horses for all that they were worth. At last we realized that it was useless to try further for the storm was almost upon us. We hurriedly unhitched the team and tied them to the sheltered side of the wagon and just got inside when that awful storm struck us. The wind blew a perfect gale, one flash of lightning followed another in such quick succession that the sky seemed filled with a blaze of light, and the roar of the thunder was deafening. We had to scream to each other to be heard. There seemed to be a lull in the storm and then it came again harder than ever because of the heavy fall of hail.

Those poor horses were so terribly frightened that they squatted down, then jumped and plunged as those awful flashes of lightning and peals of thunder came. Then the large hail stones pelting them was almost too much. Thanks to good new halter ropes, we had a team of horses after the storm was over. We were nearly as frightened as the horses. Our greatest fear was that the wind would blow the wagon over or at least tear the cover off. So we gripped the canvas tightly to try to keep it in place. Every where that our hands touched it, the water came through so that our bedding and all our clothing was sopping wet. When the storm cleared away, we saw that we were near a freshly plowed field that our road seemed to cross.

Since we did not know which way to go to find bridges if we left the road, we crossed the field. Time and again it seemed that we would mire down and not be able to go on, but those faithful little horses pulled us out each time after considerable urging on our part.

We drove up to a farm house soon after crossing the field and told the people who we were and where we were going. They were Mr. and Mrs. Todd, friends of our family who had been in our home many times. They were perfectly delightful to us. They helped us unpack our wagon, hang up our bedding and clothing to dry and then took us into their home as guests.

As Mr. Todd helped us to hitch up the colts the next morning, we were able to get an early start. We knew that our next big experience was to cross the Missouri River at Yankton, South Dakota and we wanted to get there before dark.

You know our much traveled friend, Uncle Sy, had told me that the pontoon bridge there was just two stringers so placed that when the horses walked on them the water splashed over the planks and made them hard to see. I really believed this and as we drew near the place where we were to cross I became almost hysterical with fear. I got out of the wagon and sat by the road side refusing to go any farther.

John walked down to where he could see the bridge and came back and told me that there was a good road made of planks put on flat boats and that it was perfectly safe. He did not tell me, however, that we had to ford the river for a long distance after we left the bridge.

I think he showed good judgment here for there was nothing for me to do but to ride as we followed the willow saplings that had been put in the water to mark the ford after we left the bridge.

We had camped just out of Yankton, South Dakota and John had gone to look for a place nearby where he could water the horses. I was busy getting supper while Anne tied the horses on either side of the wagon and as she was putting grain in their feed boxes she shouted, "An automobile is coming! What shall we do?" Our horses had never seen an automobile and we were not sure what they would do. We did not wonder long for the car was upon us in a moment and the horses were terribly frightened. They reared up on their hind legs and pulled at the halter ropes until we were afraid they would break loose. We foolishly thought we could quiet them by taking hold of the ropes. The horse Anne was holding reared up and threw her to the ground and stepped on her back. I rushed to her when she screamed. She is such a little thing anyway that when I saw her so white and still, I screamed and screamed for help. John came running to us. We got her up into the wagon and on the bed. Although she soon sat up and told us she was not badly hurt, we went back into Yankton and consulted with a doctor who was not too reassuring. We waited over one day to assure ourselves that Anne was only bruised and not seriously hurt. As she insisted then that she was all right and that we were foolish to wait any longer, we reluctantly started on without further delay.

I knew that we had to cross the Missouri River again at Chamberlain, South Dakota; but I had not dreaded that, for we were to ferry, and I had often crossed at Sioux City on a ferry when I was a child.

The horses were not so familiar with ferries and refused to go on the boat. Two men came and led them on for us and helped to keep them quiet while we were crossing. That ferry boat had a railing built around it with a frame work built up over the drive way. Then as the boat landed and everything was ready for us to drive off, the men let loose of the horses. They gave a great plunge up the steep slope leading away from the boat.

We heard the boatman shouting to us and we stopped to see what he wanted. He said, "Hey, Feller, the top of yer wagon is too high. It didn't miss that cross beam by mor'n a half inch." John called back, "A miss is as good as a mile," and we drove on. A short distance from the river we camped under a clump of trees near some water. This seemed the first ideal camping place that we had found. The mosquitoes apparently felt the same way about it, for soon after dark every mosquito for miles around was there and at work. We got up and built a camp fire but as the smoke would not go into the wagon where our beds were, we took turns at sleeping. One of us stayed up and kept a smudge going in a kettle. Every few minutes we would put the smudge kettle on the pitch fork and raise it up so as to let the smoke drift into the wagon and drive the mosquitoes out.

We surely looked funny the next morning. Our faces were swollen and blotched with mosquito bites and blackened with smoke until we looked like three negroes who had the measles.

For a while that morning we wished that we had a trailer for the covered wagon where some of us could ride for a while as we were too cross and disagreeable from loss of sleep to live peaceably in such close quarters, but as the day wore on we became more amiable as we anticipated the pleasure of seeing our friends in Lund that night.

They were expecting us that day, but I really think they would have been happier if we had arrived one day later for we found them just moving a shack which they had bought up by the side of their house.

They had expected us to stay several days with them and this was to be our quarters while we were there. I was eager to go right on the next morning, but my desires were over ruled by the rest of the company and it was decided that since this was Saturday, we would stay over and go to church on Sunday and start early Monday morning.

Furthermore, our friends told us they knew where they could get us a very intelligent shepherd pup that was just ready to be weaned.

I wanted a pup very much indeed so the men started off right after supper and said they would be back by early bed time. At eleven o'clock we went to bed for it seemed useless to wait up any longer as no doubt the men had been delayed for some unknown reason. About midnight I heard the puppy whine and knew that their errand had been successful.

The next morning we all got up early to see my dog. He came out toward the group of us, but as each person tried to pick him up, he ran back away from them until he came to me. He ran up to me and as I picked him up in my arms, he cuddled up like a baby. He is the dearest thing I have ever seen in the way of a dog. His hair is jet black excepting a white strip down his face, a tiny white tip on his tail and one white foot. We are constant companions.

We all went to church in a school house about five miles away on Sunday afternoon. All the men there wore overalls and the women wore wash dresses. The minister used a kitchen table for a pulpit. As there was no one else who could play the organ my friends insisted that I should play for them. It was not an easy thing to do for some the the keys on the organ would not sound, but I managed to get through after a fashion and every one seemed to appreciate my efforts. They were such kindly people we stayed at the school house and visited until so late that the sun was just setting when we got back to our friend's home.

We made preparations for an early start the next morning for the Meads in Murdo had been expecting us to come there for over a week.

We had some difficulty in getting the horses to pull the load up the first hill as we left our friends early Monday morning. John conceived the idea of shortening the tugs on the harness, which put too much weight on the horses' necks. We did not know what was the matter, but soon after noon, whenever we started up a hill, the horses would rear upon their hind legs. At each rear, I would climb out of the wagon over that chicken coop which we had fastened on the back and walk along behind the wagon for miles, carrying my pup in my apron.

We were unable to make the trip through that day, however, for when we stopped at a small town in the afternoon, John took the horses to a livery stable to water them. When he told the men about how the horses reared up when they had to pull up hill they said "Sore necks. Your tugs are too short, man!" They adjusted the tugs properly but the damage was done. Our horses had painfully sore necks and all afternoon they reared and plunged whenever they were required to make a hard pull.

We did not get into Presho until dark. We ate a scrappy lunch and got ready for the night. The wind was blowing a gale but John insisted that I must chain my pup to the wagon wheel. I did so, and the poor thing whimpered and cried like a baby.

Soon John went to a livery stable to buy some grain for the horses. While he was gone I made a nest of his sheep lined coat for my pup right by my pillow in the wagon. As soon as I put the dog into it he snuggled down and went to sleep.

John was so tired when he came in that I think he forgot all about the dog and went right to sleep. The next morning when he awoke he threw his arm across the head of the bed and struck the pup so that he yelped. John said, "Just think of it, I have slept with a dog!" He was so disgusted that he got up immediately and insisted that we start for Murdo at once.

We women folks laughed at him for being so disgruntled and refused to start until we had our breakfast. As we talked over our plans for the day, we thought it would be better for Anne and John to go on to Murdo with the wagon and for me to go on the train. They would not bother with my dog so I kept him with me, but the conductor made me put him in the baggage car. It was quite a trip for both dog and woman. The dog was so afraid of the strange men that he cried all the way. The train men were very happy to have me claim him again at Murdo.

This really was the most unique train ride that I have ever had. The railroad had only been built a short time and there was no ballast on the track. It seemed to me that the ties and rails had just been put on the prairie without any road bed judging from the lunges and jerks that the coach made as the train crept along. We went so slowly that the people riding in buggies would pass us. The men on the train would call a dinner order to the people in the

A train similar to the one Tully rode on.
(**Haaken Horizons**)

buggies and them to ask the hotel to have it ready when the train got in. Then they would get off from the rear end of the coach and run around in front and get on and come back through the aisles to make us laugh.

It was a rough ride but it was better than walking fifteen miles behind the wagon and I was very glad to reach our friends' home in Murdo. They had left word for us make ourselves at home for a couple of days as they had been called away on business, but that they would help us haul our lumber and supplies out to our homesteads if we would wait until they came back.

After supper was over, Anne and John went out to see what a new western town would be like in the evening. I begged to stay alone. The western sky gave promise of a marvelous sun set. That was much more to my liking. I was not disappointed for never have I seen more wonderful coloring. The prairie seemed to stretch so far away and I knew that we were going out there some where into that new country to build our home.

I am sure, Sara, that if that craving for our own home had been any less, I would have come back to Wakefield and my old job in the schools which the school board so generously urged me to take before we left. This pioneering had been more strenuous than I had counted on and we were far from our destination. Anne kept up such good spirits. She is such a good sport. She laughed everything off as though it were a huge joke and our whole trip was a lark to her.

Monday morning found us on the road once more. The sun came up just as we were pulling up a little hill on the way out from Murdo. Two freight wagons filled with lumber with our covered wagon following behind made up our caravan. The sleepy little town was nothing but an aggregation of make shift shacks and houses to shelter people until the rush of settlers was over and they could take time to make permanent improvements. I wondered as we were leaving Murdo if Philip would look like this, and if so, if a person could ever feel at home in such primitive surroundings.

The fifty mile trip to Anne's and Mother's filings took us two and a half days. Nothing very exciting happened on this trip only our horses necks seemed to get worse. They fretted more than ever about pulling the load up the hills. But, as I rode on one of the freight wagons, it was easier for every one not to hear me fuss.

We had two loads of lumber and our own covered wagon. It seemed that one of the three loads managed to get stuck in every bad creek crossing that we came to, but they would unhitch one or perhaps both of the other teams and hitch them on to the stalled wagon, then one of the men would shout, "One Eye! Bronch!" Then all the horses would pull and the load moved out. This delayed us so much that we did not reach mother's claim until nearly noon of the third day.

I am not happy about her claim. It is a high bench above the river and does not look like good soil. It would be fine for a part of a big ranch, but I doubt if it is worth much as a farm, but Anne has a nice piece of river bottom with plenty of timber on it. She is a lucky girl as usual. The men unloaded the lumber for the shacks and we spent the rest of the afternoon in wandering over the two homesteads.

Our friends left for Murdo the next morning before sunrise and we were making preparations for building the shacks when a rancher rode up on horse back to see if John would not help him in the hay field for two weeks.

He said he could put a sheep skin pad under the collars on our horses so their necks would heal up while they worked if we would cleanse them night and morning with some solution which he had for that purpose. He agreed to pay five dollars a day for man and team. That sounded pretty good to us for we realized that we would have much expense before the winter was over.

So it was decided that John should work in the hay and Anne and I should build the shacks. This building was great sport. Often the lifting of the lumber was more than one of us could do so we would both take a hold and together would say, "One Eye! Bronch!" and the load moved in place. "One Eye and Bronch" were the names of the horses on one of the freight wagons. No doubt you have guessed that before this.

The most difficult part of our building was putting in the windows. Mother had said, "Be sure to put one window where the light will come on the stove and another low enough so that I can see to sew." We had this in mind when we were planning our window placing,

> "One window high,
> One window low,
> Right in this corner,
> They both shall go."

We kept saying this jargon over all day as we worked. We had both windows so that they would open and shut and we felt very proud of our day's work as we went to the wagon to get our supplies preparatory to getting supper.

We loaded the things into the dishpan and each took hold of a handle of the pan and turned toward the shack. "Cross-eyed Tom," we said as with one voice. You know we had promised Tom before we left home to name the first shack that we finished for him. The corner of the house made a good nose for "Tom" and one high window and one low window gave him a fine pair of cross eyes. So Anne's shack was duly christened "Cross-eyed Tom."

We did not take so much trouble with window placement in Mother's shack but just put one long window in the front of it and we thought that she could adjust her stove and sewing chair to this window.

The rancher was mistaken for the horses necks did not get well under his treatment but got much worse. Since the shacks here were finished, we thought best to go on over to our own filing so that we would be sure to be there before our time was up on September 29th when we must establish residence.

It was difficult to know just how to plan our trips over there for it would necessitate two trips at best. At last we decided to take over our wagon load of supplies and leave them at our claim, then John would come back for the lumber. We got everything ready the night before so that we were able to get a very early start on Monday morning.

The trip across was beautiful. This is an interesting country. After traveling for some distance on a table land, you enter brakes and extremely rough country along the streams. In some instances, the streams have considerable timber along them. Then again they are like treeless ditches. We drove through large herds of cattle and horses. They did not know what about our covered wagon, and I am very sure I did not know what about them. I think all the stories I have ever heard, or read, about stampeding cattle crossed my mind as we drove along, but nothing so exciting happened. We did, however, see several mirages. They looked like small lakes not far away which disappeared, when we came up to them.

It had been so long since we had had our mail that I could scarcely wait until we came to the ranch where the post office was located; but at last we came to the top of a high hill that led down to the house. The road down it was so steep and so full of ruts that once more I lost my courage and climbed out to walk. Just as I reached the foot of the hill and started toward the gate with my little dog at my heels, I stopped suddenly, took my dog in my arms and started to run back up the hill; for right by the side of the path where I had to pass to reach the house was a large bob cat. As I ran back along the path, a friendly voice call, "Don't be afraid, lady, the cat is stuffed." I felt pretty much ashamed and turned and looked into the kindly eyes of a man who did not look like a rancher although he wore a khaki suit and high laced boots, I found out soon that he was the editor of the local paper and was only stopping at the Post Office ranch house until his temporary office was finished at Philip.

I was very glad to hear from all of you but as I read your letters I was so overwhelmed with a feeling of homesickness, I felt that it would be impossible for me to go any farther. I wanted so very much to come back home that once more I asked John if he would not consider letting me go back and reestablish our home in Wakefield. I could teach there and he could come back as he had proved up on the land.

He studied this over for a few moments and then said, "You would not go back now when we are so near the homestead without ever seeing it would you? Just think this is our chance to get a home of our own." Once more I was won over and we soon started out for fear we would not reach the homestead before dark. It was a gorgeous, bright, sunshiny day, yet the air was snappy and crisp filled with the fragrance of the dried prairie grasses.

We were obliged to pull up the long treacherous hill that I had been so afraid to ride down when we came in. Just as we reached the top of it on our way out, we saw a horseback rider coming toward us from the east. When he caught sight of us, he urged his horse into a gallop and waved his hat, evidently to attract our attention. We stopped to see what he wanted and imagine our surprise when Bill Smith from Wakefield rode up. You know he has a homestead filing adjoining ours. He had hoped to overtake us at Anne's, but when the people at the ranch told him that we had just left that morning, he rode on and overtook us here. It was fine to see some one from home. Anne was thrilled to ride his horse and we were glad to have him ride in the wagon, so that he could answer our numerous questions concerning you home folks.

We soon reached Philip on Bad River, and it did not look at all as I had pictured it, as is usually the case when you anticipate anything for a long time. The real picture is quite likely to be different.

Philip is built where the North and South Forks of Bad River come together. The Bad River has some timber on it but so far there are no bridges. The water was very shallow where we forded, but the pitch was so steep getting in and out of the ford that the horses slipped and backed the wagon down into the water when we were trying to pull out. I suppose their necks hurt so badly that they hated to pull, but after backing down several times they finally reached the top.

There is a lodging house and a few shacks near the bank of the river. I wanted to camp there and come on the next day but the men hooted at that idea when we were only about six or seven miles from our destination. It was necessary for us to go as far as the store anyway, for we were short of provisions. This was about a mile further on the bank of the North Fork.

The store is much like any cross roads general store, just one large room to accomodate a mixed stock of goods. There is a small lean-to at the back for oil barrels. The whole thing is just boarded up and covered with tar paper. But the people who run that store are cultured and refined. They evidently are southerners and have two of the most adorable children. The girl is about eight with beautiful brown eyes and long brown curls. The boy is about six I should say, with brown eyes and golden curls that come down to his shoulders. I fell in love with them at once. They came up and talked to me. I think Mrs. Jenkins must have sensed my pleasure for she asked me to come over to the house and chat while the men shopped.

Her home is my ideal of a ranch home. It is built of logs and has a small bay window in the living room. It was a real treat to sit in a comfortable chair and talk about something besides the ordeal of living in a covered wagon, and the difficulties attendant upon traveling with horses that had sore necks. She had many of the recent magazines on the table in the living room. They looked so good to me that I think I could have eaten them. She must have sensed the hungry look in my eyes for she very tactfully gave me the latest "Ladies Home Journal" when we left. With this precious treasure in my arms the prospect of more miles in the covered wagon seemed tolerable.

The crossing at North Fork was dreadful! We got stuck in the mud and even after Bill hitched his saddle horse on to help pull, the horses could not budge the load. A kindly man came toward us driving a great big team of dapple grays. He offered to help us and we were most happy to accept his offer and were soon on our way.

As we pulled out upon the flat above the breaks of Bad River, we saw a small tar paper shack on our left that for some reason interested me immensely. Perhaps it was because I caught a glimpse of the lovely face of a white-haired woman at the window. I want to go back there.

On our right was a square log house that the men say is the school house. Maybe I shall teach there some day. Who knows? The men were anxious to get to a ranch where they had stayed when there were here in March and filed on the land. They said that we could get fresh milk and eggs there and that it was the easiest way to our filing. They did not say, however, that we had to ford the South Fork of Bad River to get there. Perhaps it was just as well for the ford was not bad at all and just as we were pulling up on the far side, we scared up six grouse that lighted in some brush not far away. John took his gun and went after them. I think he must have had "buck fever" for he came back empty handed, and I cried. Such a silly thing for a grown woman to do, but our diet had been so much the same for almost two months that perhaps a few tears were justified.

The men were thoroughly disgusted with me and we drove to the ranch in silence, only to find no one at home. We were a disappointed group as we started on west to the homesteads. It was nearly sundown, the shadows were long so I walked behind the wagon with my dog and Anne cantered ahead riding Bill's black saddle horse. The sun was a golden red ball that seemed to rest on the top of a ridge of hills. As we climbed up and up, I kept saying to myself, "On, on into the sunset."

It was beginning to get dusk as we came up to the top of a high ridge of hills where we could look off to the west and see the sloping bench land that led down to Meyer's draw. This, the men told me was our homestead, but that it would be best not to attempt to ford Meyer's draw that night as the crossing was bad. So we made camp once more but this time we were in sight of the promised land. The wind that blew hard all night made the wagon creak and kept the canvas flapping until it was difficult to sleep. Still I awoke quickly when all this noise stopped as the wind died down at dawn.

Anne scolded about the dust over everything as we were getting our hasty breakfast, but the dust did not bother me for I was so entranced with the odor of the dried prairie grass that filled the early morning air, and my eagerness to get over to our own homestead so that we might choose the place where we were to build our first home.

John and I started to walk on over as soon as we had finished breakfast. Anne said that she would "break camp" and Bill said that he would catch up the horses and bring the load on over later. He did not seem to have any sentiment about coming to his homestead to build a home. Perhaps the reason for this is that he and Jane Anderson have decided to wait until he proves up before they are married. He told us this yesterday when I told him that I hoped that he would bring her with him when he came to establish his residence.

John and I were like two happy children as we crossed Meyer's draw and John said, "Now this is our land." I slipped my hand in his and walked for a short distance without saying anything. Then we came to the slope of a side hill that made me think of my old home in Kansas and I gave little squeals of delight and said, "John, John this is just where we will live. We will put the house right here." John just grinned. He did not say anything until I had calmed down a little bit and then he said, "This place will be all right as far as I am concerned, if there is any water near here."

We found a large water hole just a short distance away and enough dry wood near by to last for a short time. These things made it possible for John to carry out his plan of leaving early this morning to go back to Anne's place for our lumber. I do not expect him back until sometime tomorrow.

Wait a minute, here he comes, right now! The dog just barked and when I looked out what should I see but John coming with the lumber, so I shall cut this short. How he ever made that trip over to Anne's place and back in a day I am sure I can't understand, but here he is.

We found the camp fires and gasoline stoves impractical here where there is so much wind and so we bought a sheet iron camp stove from the rancher near Anne's place. I can get a hot fire in it in just a few minutes.

I'll leave this now and get some hot coffee ready for John by the time he gets here. He must be tired and hungry, poor dear.

Much love to you all.
Tully

Our New Home

November 15, 1906

My dear Sara:

At last we are in our new home, but the building of it was been fraught with many difficulties. The finished product is a sod structure and dug out, covered with a car roof. That is a roof such as you see on freight cars. The room is twenty feet long, fourteen feet wide and eight feet high. It faces south with one window in the east and one window and the door in the south. The north wall is in the bank, the east and west walls are partially in the bank and partly sod, the south side is all of sod.

It was rather difficult to decide that we should make a dug-out for John thought we could not live in one. You remember, Sara, that grandmother's pioneer home in Iowa was on the side hill with the back kitchen and cellar underground. Yet on the same level with the kitchen which made me feel that I, too, wanted a semi-dug out. Mother said their pioneer home in Kansas was partly a dug out, and here we are in our dug out. The most practical reason that a dug out would be best for us was that when John got back with our lumber that we had left at Anne's, some one had taken part of it. There was scarcely enough left for a very small shack above ground.

Mr. Alexander, who has a big ranch over on South Fork, came past today and told me that we have been very foolish to put our house here on the side hill for during the winter the snow will blow off the flat above the house and make a huge drift in our door yard. I surely hope that he is mistaken for it has been hard work to build this house and we are as "comfy" as can be in here. It will be easy to heat and as fuel will be scarce, this is quite an item in the dug out's favor. I do not really relish the idea of freezing to death even if it were to happen in "our new home." It has taken us two months to build this place, for we have had so many interruptions.

The day we decided where to locate the house, Anne and I put on overalls and we dug out the dirt and loaded it on the wheel barrow while the men wheeled it away. We were just getting along fine when late in the afternoon we saw some people drive up on Bill's place. He has borrowed a tent and sleeps on his own place but takes his meals here with us. We were indeed surprised when the people came on over where we were at work and we found it was our friends from Lund. Food was rather scarce for such a large crowd of us, so I hurried the men off to the store in Philip. Fortunately for all concerned, the freight wagons had just arrived from Pierre with plenty of food. When John and Bill returned they brought canned sweet potatoes, pork and beans, tomatoes, beans and hominy, also a few potatoes, onions, and some bacon.

I was not long in preparing a meal of tomatoes, fresh fried potatoes and onions. I thought when I looked at all the food the men had brought that it would last for a week, but we are not satisfied with an ordinary amount of food here. We eat quantities of it. When our friends left us on Monday, our food supply was very low again.

A sod house, similar to the one Tully
*and her husband built. (*Haaken Horizons*)*

It had been fine to have them with us, but we had been unable to do any work on the house while they were here. We tried to make up for lost time by all of us working doubly hard on Tuesday. Wednesday Bill went to the mail box for our mail. When he came home in the evening, he a letter from Mother saying that she would be in Murdo Friday and expected some of us to be there to meet her. That came like a "thunderbolt out of a clear sky." We were not expecting her for two weeks and had planned to get our house done in the meantime.

Murdo was seventy miles away and our horses had those dreadfully sore necks. Of course, some one had to go for Mother, so we decided that John should go and take Anne back to her place, which was on his way, for she needed to be there to keep her residence valid. Bill was to go to Philip the next day and get more provisions for him and me. Then he was to help me with the house building, or more properly, house digging.

John went to one of the neighbors and explained our situation to them and they loaned him a small tent for me to use while he was gone. We set up the tent near the place where we were digging our house, took the bed springs out of the covered wagon and set them up on tomato cans, for this tent was to be my house while they were away. Since John was planning to bring back our winter's supply of food, I thought he would probably be gone five or six days.

When I saw them all disappear over the hill the next morning, my heart sank. I was afraid of this big, strange out doors. The range cattle and horses roamed at will all around me, and I had no food left excepting one small can of cove oysters.

This was no time for self pity for apparently I was the only person to work on the house that day so I set to work. The forenoon was hot and those wheel barrows full of dirt were about all I could manage. I would haul out three and then lie down on the cool moist ground in the shade of the wall for fifteen minutes and then go to work again. At half past eleven, I quit work so that I would be rested enough to get dinner for I was sure Bill would be back by twelve, and still no Bill. Then I decided to eat the can of oysters and get him something else when he got there. Unfortunately the oysters were not good and a few minutes after I had eaten them, I was taken violently ill.

The afternoon was long and hot as I lay in the shade and bathing my face with a damp cloth to keep me from fainting, praying that some one would come, but no one came, not even Bill.

When it grew cooler toward evening, I felt better and took a camp stool up to the top of the hill to watch the sun set and perhaps see some one coming. My little dog seemed to sense my loneliness for he made queer little noises as he lay curled up in my lap. Maybe it was only dog talk but at any rate it helped to break the stillness. A soft breeze had been blowing all day but it died down at sun set. The stillness was so intense that it hurt. Then the katydids began to sing and I think I was never more pleased to hear any church choir. The night hawks swooped too near my head for comfort. I did not know what they were and they frightened me. When a few stars appeared in the sky, I felt sure that this was to be a supperless night for me, but I waited there on the hill until the sky was ablaze with stars and the friendly moon made it a perfect night. It did not seem that God could be far away, so I went into the tent and made a bed on the floor beside mine for my dog. I think I must have gone to sleep right away, for I knew nothing more until I was roused by the dog's barking back of the tent. I got up and looked out in time to see a bunch of range horses galloping in the opposite direction with the dog at their heels. The stars seemed so very near, the sky was brilliant with them but the stillness all around was oppressive until the yip, yip of a coyote away to the south told me that there were at least wild things living in this great out doors. My dog came back soon, and I crept back into bed, but did not sleep any more. I got up before sun up and dug for little while on the house, but I was too weak to work long and my head ached violently.

I knew there were neighbors a mile or so away but since I have no sense of direction and could not see a house, I feared to start away from our camp for fear I would be lost on the open prairie.

Noon came and went and I was too hungry and ill to work any longer so I lay down in the shade hoping that some one would drive past so that they could get help for me, when I heard hoof beats and here came Bill as smiling and happy as though he had arrived twenty four hours earlier. When he saw how ill I looked he was quite conscious stricken for all the food he had brought was some bacon and some crackers. He scarcely waited to explain that as he did not realize that I was without food, he had gone several miles north of Philip to look at some land that he had heard was exceptionally fine, then he dashed off to the store and this time brought food enough to last until John got home. He seemed to want to make amends for his thoughtlessness for he suggested that we put the roof on our partly finished dug out so that we could have shelter in case of a storm. I readily agreed to this proposal and by noon of the second day we had used up all the lumber we had and felt quite well satisfied, for John was to bring more lumber when he came.

That night about midnight the dog dashed out of the tent barking furiously. I listened and heard the creak of a wagon in the distance. I was terribly frightened then all at once I heard John's familiar "whoo who!" I did not even think of rattle snakes as I rushed out of the tent and down to the creek crossing wearing my bathrobe and bed room slippers. The moon light was so bright that I could see there were two people in the wagon. Sure enough there was my darling, little mother.

The joy of seeing her was somewhat clouded when she said that she was having difficulty with her filing and that it would be necessary for her to go to Belvedere to complete her records. Belvedere was about seventy miles southeast of us. It seemed a shame for her to ride that far in a lumber wagon, so we borrowed a buggy, harness, and one horse from neighbors. Bill very kindly offered his horse and said that he would be glad to make the drive so that he could see the country.

They were off the next morning just at sunrise and John and I started to work on the house. Then I realized what a mistake it had been to put the roof on before we had finished digging for it was so hard to work in cramped quarters, but by night we had made quite a showing. We had one end of the house dug deep enough to move our beds inside so that it was more comfortable for mother when she returned. She was such a good sport that she seemed much more concerned with the effort we had put forth for her comfort than she did with the fatigue she must have felt after her long hard drive.

She had the blood of the pioneer in her veins for my grandmother and grandfather had pioneered in Iowa. They came from Michigan and when they reached the place where Chicago now stands, my grandmother was so tired from riding on the ox cart that she begged grandfather to stop there. "What, settle here on this swamp. I should say not. We are going on out to the rich plains of Iowa." This was my grandfather's ultimatum. They settled in Linn County, Iowa and later at Shell Rock in Butler County where they built log houses, a saw mill and a grist mill.

My father was a northern soldier in the civil war. Soon after the war was over, he and my mother were married. There was much talk of the opportunities for young folks in western Kansas where they could file on a homestead and a timber claim. The urge of the pioneer stock was strong and they went into western Kansas and built their sod house on their homestead filing which joined the timber claim.

Mother seemed so thrilled to think that we were making a sod dug out that I sometimes wondered if she were not glad that our lumber had been stolen. No doubt she was living again her early life as a Kansas pioneer. The past usually is pleasant to contemplate for the hardships resolve themselves into adventures as time moves on. She enjoyed our bustling about and always found some good reason for staying on when we suggested taking her home.

The weather was perfect with crisp, cold mornings, changing into balmy noon day with an early sun set, no twilight, but the most beautiful starry heavens, the sky a turquoise blue just ablaze with stars that seemed so near that I used to call them friends. Each morning just before sunrise a gentle breeze would spring up carrying with it the fragrance of the grasses. No perfume was ever sweeter, and no air fresher or more invigorating. Some days the breeze died down at sunrise, again it would grow into a gale, which usually stopped at sunset.

This marvellous climate coupled with the manual labor we were doing gave us enormous appetites and we were making great inroads on our provisions which we had hoped would last us all winter.

When it was necessary for mother to go to her homestead to establish residence, Bill offered to take her over for he had heard of a shack that he could buy very cheaply and he could take this opportunity to go and see it. We rejoiced with him on his return when he said he would not need to make a dug out as he had bought this shack he would move over to his place. He would just sod it on the outside. This would make it comfortable for him as long as he would need to live there to prove up. Bill said he was in no hurry to move his shack over, but would gladly help us with our house and also our barn if he could take his meals with us until the work was finished.

A friendly neighbor who had settled several miles west of us came over one day and offered us his scraper so that we could dig more rapidly. We started the barn at once. This seemed like a god-send for as yet, we had no shelter for our horses or chickens. It was only a matter of a few days to dig out a place for a barn and a hen house with this scraper and a team, but we could not use them on the house for that roof and front wall of dirt which we were leaving made their use impractical.

When John filed on our place in March there were several large trees on Meyers' draw and some on a short draw on the place, but when we came in September, these had all been cut down with one or two exceptions. In some cases, some of the large limbs were still on the ground. One tree had been cut so recently that the leaves were still green on the branches that had been trimmed off. After much deliberation, we decided to cut down the only very large tree left standing and use what poles we needed to add to the supply that the former wood cutters had left to make a pole roof for the barn. After we had the poles in place we covered them with hay and then a layer of dirt and our stock had shelter for the winter. We hauled the rest of the tree up to the house and it furnished the major portion of our fuel for the winter.

The men had taken time to cut some hay over on our south quarter, but we realized by now that we were not going to be able to do all that was necessary to be done before winter over took us so we bought a stack of hay about six miles away which we hoped to haul as soon as we had the house finished.

The days were getting much shorter and colder, so we attacked our house building again. After digging it out inside, we made a sod wall along the south and east and west up to the eaves. The roof at the north rested on the bank. The last day that we worked at it was a cloudy, raw day. We finished just at dark as a sleet storm started. We were very happy to be cozily settled in our house, and felt a great sense of relief to know that our horses were sheltered also, as we heard a storm drive across the roof late that night.

The cold weather moderated toward morning and the snow and sleet turned to rain. About daylight something wakened me. As I raised up on my elbow and looked about, I began to cry for our sod wall on the south side had caved out and I realized that all this hard work must be done over. The water from the eaves had washed down on the sod before it had settled and the sod caved away. Fortunately I had brought a rag carpet with me. We nailed that up to keep out the cold until we could repair the damage.

I had breakfast about ready when we heard voices outside. Mr. and Mrs. Wilson and Mrs. Scales had come to see if they could stay with us for a few days until they could get their shack built. They had just arrived on their land the day before. The storm during the night had made them fearful of camping out.

Such was pioneering. They had no home at all and we had little enough to offer to them. They stayed with us a day or so, then they decided to go back to their relatives in the Bad Lands and not try to build their house until later, as they did not need to be on their land until March.

We were several days in repairing the damages done to our house, but we are now comfortably housed and almost ready for winter.

Lovingly,

Tully

Our First Winter

February 25, 1907

My dear Sara:

Our kindly "Uncle Sam" says that we homesteaders need stay only eight months on these homesteads before we can prove up. He surely is a wise old man if this winter that we have just lived through is any sample of South Dakota winters.

We seldom ever go away from the place. I am afraid to ride in the wagon and I do not like to have John go away and leave me here alone. Bill Smith took your last letter to the post office for me and when he came home he said very casually, "Have you seen any strange men riding around here today?"

"No, why?"

"Did you see any yesterday?"

"No! Why all this mystery? What has happened?"

His non-committal air irritated me. "Oh, I don't know as anything has happened but they told me down at the store that a criminal had escaped from the jail in Fort Pierre and that the officers had followed him out into the brakes along Meyer's draw, there they lost his trail. I thought you might have seen them riding around here some where."

I told John that I was afraid the man would come to the house for food. He just laughed at me and said, "That man is not staying around in these parts. He is miles away long before this." This silenced me, but did not convince me that he was right.

On the following Monday morning he and Bill left very early to get a load of hay from a stack that we had bought down on the South Fork river bottom. I knew they were going several miles away but I was not sure just how far, for as they drove away I asked how long they would be gone. They said, "Oh we don't know exactly. It is several miles over there."

They had been gone only a short time when my little dog barked loudly. I heard a man's voice call, "Any body to home?" I went to the door and my heart almost stood still for there stood the trampiest looking man. He had on dirty, torn overalls; his face was dirty and unshaven; his brown eyes were crossed and they had an ugly look in them as they peered out at me from beneath a dirty, torn cap brim. I felt sure that this was the criminal who had succeeded in evading the officers. I summoned all of my school ma'am dignity and said, "Good morning. What do you want may I ask?"

Ignoring my question he said, "Any men folks to home?"

"Not just at this moment, but I trust they will be soon, they are over hill after a load of hay." This was a "white lie" for it was only part of the truth. They had gone over not only one hill but many hills, and I had no idea when they would return.

He tried to brush past the dog and come inside, but the dog stood his ground and growled so fiercely that the man asked to come in, saying he had been sent by one of the ranchers near by to see my husband on business. He came in and sat down near the stove while

I took a chair at some distance from him with my dog sitting squarely on my feet.

Conversation with my strange guest was most difficult. He grew tired of waiting and moved uneasily in his chair. This only added to his discomfort, for every time he moved the dog would show his teeth and growl as much as to say, "Stay where you are, please." My guest told me again and again that I was harboring a vicious dog. I assured him just as often that the dog only behaved that way when there were strange men on the place.

He gave me such an ugly look when I said this that I trembled all over. The dog seemed to sense that something was wrong for he drew back his lips, and gave a wicked growl and then crouched on my feet as though he were going to spring at the stranger.

At this the man quickly put his hand into his hip pocket. I thought he was going to shoot and I am sure every particle of color left my face. I could not get out of doors unless I passed very near where the man was seated and I wondered how much longer this agony would be prolonged, when the man drew a dirty old wallet from his hip pocket and took a watch out of it. He scrutinized it for several minutes, it seemed to me, and then said, "I think it is past noon and them men 'aint come yet. I guess I'll have to be goin', so I can just as well tell you what I want. I wonder if your husband won't come over to my place and do some plowin' for me before the ground freezes too hard."

I told him that we had far more work to do than we would be able to get done but if my husband felt that he could his work, he would come over to see him. So this man was only a neighbor and I had suffered in agony for hours thinking that I was entertaining a desperate criminal.

As soon as he was gone and I was alone with my precious dog, I hugged him again and again, and told him that I might come from pioneer stock, but I was not a brave pioneer. I was simply a coward, almost afraid of my own shadow. Those men came home with the hay about dark, hungry and cross. When I told them about my strange guest they manifested no interest whatever.

Perhaps it was just as well for when we awoke the next morning the ground was covered with about eighteen inches of snow. It changed the looks of things completely. All the familiar hills and landmarks were gone and in their places were these strange white mounds. As this made plowing impossible, our neighbor's visit was fruitless.

Our mail box was on a star route about three miles away. The day before was mail day and I was most anxious for news from the home folks. Remembering my strange guest of the day before, I decided to go with John for the mail. He said the snow was too deep for me but I insisted on trying. I walked behind him and stepped in his foot steps. We had gone about a mile of the way when it seemed that my hip came out of place. Such a predicament!

I insisted that John should go on and get the mail while I started for home. It was a slow and painful journey. He made the return trip in time to help me across the creek and up to the house. My hip was so painful that I was obliged to stay in bed for a few days and it has bothered me off and on all winter. The mail brought a letter from Mother saying that she and Ann were coming over to have Thanksgiving dinner with us, and that they were bringing a turkey. A turkey! Whoopee!!

I had not told John that I was dreading for Thanksgiving to come for I could not bear to think of spending that day alone in our little, dark, dreary, lonely dugout, with bacon as our meat dish for Thanksgiving dinner. Bacon, bacon, bacon, we had been eating nothing but bacon for months. Now everything was different. We were going to have a regular Thanksgiving dinner for we were going to have turkey and best of all Mother and Anne would be with us.

They said that we did not need to come for them as they had made other arrangements about coming over. This gave an air of mystery to their visit for we could not imagine how they could come over when they had no team or any other means of getting about. Mother had said in her letter that she would bring everything for the dinner, but I was so eager to do my share that I soaked out some dried corn to cook. I put on the finishing touches by getting up early on Thanksgiving morning and making a pumpkin pie, canned pumpkin, and fixing some onions to cream, and some potatoes to mash for dinner.

After that was done, I sat by the east window and watched "the pass" so that I might see them when they first came in sight. I did not have long to wait that morning for about ten o'clock here they came in grand style. They were able to hire a team and buggy from a man at the ranch where John had worked in the hay earlier in the fall.

Mother had fixed cranberry jelly and oyster dressing of cove oysters besides the turkey and we had a grand Thanksgiving dinner. I am sure no other four people ever consumed as much food as we did that day. There was not a bit of turkey left. It was just wonderful to have Mother and Anne, and they had planned to stay until the next day. How splendid!

The next afternoon came all too soon and as I saw them disappear over the hill in the distance, I could not keep the tears back. It was lonely here and mother had said that they probably would not come over again until Spring on account of the danger from storms. We could not get away for we had the chickens and a cow.

I must tell you how we got the cow. John had seen an auction sale bill when he was down at the store one day. It advertised some good milk cows, so we decided to go down to the sale.

This was my first trip away from the homestead since we landed. The sale was advertised for one o'clock on Saturday afternoon. We had an early lunch and John came in soon and said he had the team ready to start. He was dressed in a blue shirt and overalls. I refused to go unless he would dress up. So much against his will he put on his black suit, white shirt, dress overcoat, and hat; while I dolled myself up in my black suit with the extremely long skirt, my white flannel blouse and big white hat.

I admit I felt a little queer dressed like this riding in a lumber wagon, but oh horrors! When we got there we had to go out into the dirty corral with the cows! We picked out a cow that suited us, and were able to get her for the price we could pay. The men put a halter on her and tied her to the back of the wagon and we started, but the cow didn't. She set all four feet firmly on the ground and she shook her head and bawled. I got out and took a stick and attempted to make her lead. Imagine me in all that finery, that long black skirt sweeping the dirt, and my white hat over one ear. I was quite determined, but so was the cow. At last, Mr. Jenkins at the store told us to put the cow in the corral and come with a saddle horse and probably she would lead. The next day Bill and John went down on horse back and got her.

I am not sure that I ever want those people to see me again after my rediculous appearance. But how did I know what a cattle auction was like. I had never seen one. There seems to be so much to learn and I know so very little about all this. It is quite another world from what we are used to.

John has made me some adorable rustic furniture for the house. At least I think it is. He cut limbs from a tree that have a crotch on them for bed posts. We put poles across for side and end rails and nailed them in place. These hold the bed springs and I think the whole thing is good looking. He made me a rustic chair much the same way. I have it padded with a comforter and a pillow and it is quite comfortable.

The wood and water question is like the proverbial poor "always with us." The second Saturday in December we had been working all day getting out drift wood for kindling and we were just coming home when we saw a wagon stop at our house.

We hurried along to see who all the people were when we found that it was Mother, Anne, sister-in-law Beth and the two babies, my brother-in-law Harry Gladman and his father. The men had come up looking for homesteads. Mother knew of two claims near us so they had come over to look at them. This was a jolly reunion. Mother brought a huge roast of beef and Beth brought two loaves of home made bread. They knew I would not be prepared to get supper for eleven people without any notice. They also brought lots of bedding so that we were able to make fairly comfortable beds on the floor for some of us. We talked away into the night. Our crowded quarters and uncomfortable beds did not seem to dampen our ardor for visiting.

The men each found a piece of land that suited them the next day and we began to talk of plans for their return trip. They had driven my brother's big team over and it was finally arranged that Anne should stay with me and John take Mother, Beth and her two babies back to their homesteads and then take Harry G. and his father on to Murdo where they could take the train back to their homes. John was to bring back some more provisions for all of us and then Anne would drive my brother's team back home.

The men took turns at cutting wood so that we would have plenty of fuel while John was gone. Mother made us promise that we would carry the wood into the house and rick it up against the wall so we would be safe in case it should storm.

The next day was cloudy and cool. We thought it would be fine to go grouse hunting. Anne was a fine shot with the rifle. As the men had told her that she could not shoot a grouse with the rifle, we went out to prove that they were wrong. They were mistaken for she shot one. We had gone so far that it was almost dark when we got home and as it was beginning to rain we attacked the woodpile with a vengeance. Once more we played we were "One Eye and Bronch" and did not stop until we had the wood all carried into the house and all the chores done. I suggested that we should tie the clothes line to the corner of the house and to the corner of the barn so that we could get back and forth in case the storm turned in a blizzard.

It was after dark when we finally finished with our work and went into the house to get supper. The storm was increasing and we congratulated ourselves on getting all the wood into the house as we heard the snow continuously sweeping across the roof and we realized that a blizzard was raging.

My dog and I had been constant companions from the day we got him when he was six weeks old. I had never treated him like a dog but more like a child. I talked with him in a conversational tone and he seemed to know ever word I said. I called him Blucher. He had his own dishes for his food and his own bed at night. But he liked best of all a small upholstered foot stool which I had brought with us in the covered wagon. When I would say, "Blucher, let us have a visit," he would go and get upon his foot stool and turn his head from one side to the other as though he were listening to what I was saying. Anne also liked the foot stool for her feet, when she was reading or sewing. She was trying to read on this particular evening but Blucher wanted the foot stool. He nosed her feet until she lifted them off the stool and then he climbed up on it and sat there just like a stubborn child.

When it came time for him to go to bed he whined pitifully, lay down for a few minutes, then got up and walked around whining. He seemed to have a cold so I put a hot water bottle on his chest and one on his back and he quieted down and went to sleep, but soon after we had gone to sleep, he wakened us with pitiful whining. I got up and built the fire and heated water for the water bottles again. This performance was repeated many times during the night. Each time Anne would protest for fear I would burn up all the kindling. My efforts were rewarded for the dog got easier and towards morning he went to sleep and so did I. We did not waken until almost nine o'clock. I raised up and looked at the clock. The luminous dial showed nine o'clock, but the room was very dark. Then I realized that what the rancher friend had told us was all too true. Our home was built on the wrong side of the hill. The north west wind had blown the snow across the flat land above the house and piled it into a huge snow drift covering the house. We were frightened for we did not know how deeply we were buried nor how long our air supply would last.

As neither of us wished to alarm the other one unduly we hurriedly got our breakfast and laid our plans for getting out in order to feed the stock although we feared that the storm was still raging. Both of us bundled up like Eskimos, Anne had on one of John's short over coats with a pair of his long woolen socks pulled on over her shoes and with my hood and scarf bundled around her head and my fur mittens on, she thought she could brave the storm. We tied a long rope around her waist and I was to stay inside the house and hold one end of the rope so as to pull her back if she had any difficulty. When we opened the door, we just stood and looked at each other for we were facing a wall of snow. Since the roof of the house was practically flat we thought if we could get out on the roof we could walk over the drift to the barn. Accordingly we put the foot stool on a chair and a box on the stool. Anne mounted these and I was to stand on the chair and push her through a hole in the top of the drift which we had made with the hoe, bringing the snow down into the house and putting it in the wash tub and boiler.

> *"The best laid plans of mice and men*
> *Gang aft aglee."*

I pushed and pushed until Anne kicked me so hard I brought her down only to find that I had been shoving her head first into the snow bank. Our little plan did not work.

The storm was still raging. We thought it best to wait until it abated before we tried again to get out.

Snowstorms easily turned life threatening.
(Haaken Horizons)

Bucher laid quietly on his bed and slept, so Anne had the foot stool without controversy. Perhaps that is why she so willingly read aloud to me all day while I sewed. Maybe we both felt that this was the easiest way to hide our anxiety from each other.

Where was John during this awful storm? Would he be caught out on the open prairie and perish? What of Mother in her little shack alone? Would she have wood enough to keep from freezing? What of my sister-in-law in her little shack with her two babies and my brother away at work? Did she have enough fuel and food to last her through the storm? How long could we live under this huge snow drift. Would our frail roof hold up the weight of snow that seemed to be piling up on it? Would our stock freeze to death, or die from hunger and thirst before we could get to them? These ugly thoughts chased themselves back and forth through my brain until I fear I was not an intelligent listener, but we did not discuss our thoughts with each other. It seemed best to do other things to occupy our minds if possible and trust that Divine Love would care for us and our loved ones.

About three o'clock in the afternoon, Anne suddenly stopped reading and we said as with one voice, "It's stopped!" Sure enough the wind had died down and we knew now that we could get out of the house. Once more we bundled up like Eskimos. This time we took the hoe and brought the snow down into the house until we had an inclined plane that led to the top of the drift. We walked out and up to the top of the house. Then how we laughed for it seemed that all the snow in the country was over and in front of our buildings. We could even see patches of bare ground on the flat above the house.

We hurried down and dug a hole in the drift that covered the barn. Anne slid down into the barn and I carried the hay to her. We gave the stock an extra good feed of grain to make up for their long fast. It was more difficult to water them for we had to carry the water to them as we could not get them out of the barn.

By taking turns at the shoveling we were able to make five steps in the snow drift leading down into the house. We called these our marble stairs and carried tubs full of snow up out of the house until we could get the door shut. We felt quite proud of our efforts, for mother and grandmother had told many stories of their pioneering days, but they had never been snowed in as we had.

The excitement of doing all this and getting our hearty supper carried us well over into the evening. Then as night settled down so still and cold we talked very earnestly of the grave danger that faced the other members of our family. There seemed to be nothing for us to do that night. Perhaps we could get help in the morning. We did not dare to leave the place at night for fear of getting lost. About nine o'clock we heard a friendly "whoo who." I said, "That is John" and started for the door. Anne tried to hold me back saying, "You don't know who that is. Watch out!" I was so sure that it was John that I opened the door wide, and heard his kindly voice say, "Where are you? Are you all right? How can I get in?" By this time he had seen the light which led him to our marble stairs and he came down into the room. His coming seemed an answer to my prayers. If ever a man was needed it was right now. He told us that everything was all right with all the family, and also that the storm was really not so bad on the upland. He had brought a wagon load of provisions. Some of these he left at my brother's, some with my mother, and the rest were for us. They were on the wagon which he had left a mile or so back on the prairie.

The snow had obliterated the road and he was just driving across the country guiding himself by the stars. As he neared our place the country began to get rough and he was afraid to attempt to come any further without a light and so he had come home after the lantern.

I gave him a good hot supper and then went back with him after the load. We found everything as he had left it. The horses blanketed and tied to the back of the wagon. They seemed contented after having eaten the grain out of the nose bags. These horses of my brother's were so large that I felt like a little girl as I went ahead with the lantern following the trail that we had made as we came over.

Anne left early the next morning for we both felt that she should get back to Mother although John assured us that she would be all right. When our rancher friends saw the storm coming up, they knew that Mother was alone and had gone up and taken her down to the ranch house where she was as comfortable and happy as could be. John had left her there when he came on over home.

The terrible fear of getting lost is always with me. I am afraid to venture out of sight of our buildings so my walks usually are to a hill across a small draw from the house. The great expanse of land stretching away in all directions with only Bill Smith's shack in sight, often makes me feel that we are out of civilization. Yet there is seldom a day passes that there is not some one at the house for a meal. I could not quite understand this at first. The cowboys would ride up, drop the bridle reins over the horse's heads, and visit with John until the meal was ready; and then, as in the custom of this country, they stayed to eat.

The informality of it all is very pleasant and we have met some interesting people. One young chap is from Chicago. That is, the family lived in Chicago until he was grown, then the father decided to come west and start a cattle ranch. The mother was a good musician and had helped this oldest son to get a fairly good musical education. Her only regret in leaving Chicago was that his musical education would be interrupted. The call of the west was too strong for the father to resist, so the family came over land in two covered wagons and settled on a ranch about four miles from us. They put up a log house and barn and were just getting things arranged like a home should be, when the mother was taken with typhoid fever and died.

The task of home maker fell on this chap's young shoulders and he has done a very splendid job of it. He taught me how to make sour dough bread and pan cakes. The pan cakes are not bad, but the bread tastes sour. It is much better than no bread at all and we do get tired of baking powder biscuits. Besides it is a difficult matter for me to keep enough yeast and baking powder on hand for I do not seem to be able to plan for all this extra cooking.

Baking powder and yeast were not the only things that were running low. Our stock of provisions seemed to melt away. By Christmas I felt we would be obliged to economize in some way or we would be hungry before the roads were passable for John to make another trip to Murdo.

Other people seemed to be in the same circumstances, for Mrs. Arnot, one of the neighbor ladies came over and asked me if I would be willing to prepare a part of the Christmas dinner and let her prepare a part and the two families would spend the day together at her home. This seemed a very pleasant arrangement and I said that for part of my share I would furnish the chicken. This pleased her very much for they had not had any chicken since they came into the homestead country several months before.

The day before Christmas we caught the chickens and to our great surprise they were as light as feathers. We killed one and it was so poor that it was not fit to cook. I was non-plussed. If I could not furnish chicken we had no other meat to take. John arose to the occasion and took his gun and went out to get some grouse, but there were no grouse to be found so he came home late that night with two nice young rabbits. These were a god send to me. We dressed them and hung them up to cool. The next morning I got up early and stuffed them, stripped with bacon, and baked them.

I was very much pleased with this contribution and thought John was a good sport to save the day for me. I had not counted on the fact that all people do not like rabbit.

When we arrived at our neighbor's home about noon and I began unpacking my baskets of food, I told my chicken story. One of the little boys began to cry and said, "But you said you would bring chicken." I tried to soothe him by saying, "Yes, I know I did, but the chickens were so poor that they were not fit to eat, and so I have brought some rabbits that are nice and fat and tender." The older boy looked at me incredulously and said, "That's what you say. I know that any kind of chicken would taste good to me. I am just starved for chicken." That was too much for me. All the anticipated pleasure vanished for the day. We ate in comparative silence. We older folks ate of the rabbit and attempted forced jokes, but the kiddies refused meat and ate very sparingly of the other food. It seemed that they had wakened very early that morning and had taken turns watching for us to come to bring chicken for dinner.

Do you think it is quite fair to bring children into these out of the way places so that they lose practically all the joy out of childhood? The experience with the chickens being so thin made us more concerned about the horses. They were both thin but our Phoebe horse was alarmingly so.

The ranchers tell us that it sometimes takes a year for stock to get acclimated in this country. We had been feeding grain but it cost so much that we were very doubtful if we would have money enough to buy an increasing amount of grain. Yet we could not risk losing either of our horses and so we continued to buy grain feed for them.

January was a blustery, stormy month with a heavy fall of snow. You know Mother's birthday is February third. I had hoped that she and Anne would come over and spend her birthday with us, but during the night of February first the wind came up from the northwest and in the morning our house was once more buried under a snow drift, with a very heavy drift on the northwest corner of the roof. In fact, the weight of the snow had bowed the boards down until it seemed that they would break with the weight of it. Then, too, as our dimension timbers had not been long enough when we built the house, we put a 2x4 in the center of the room and one on either side and nailed the roof scantlings to them. If they once slipped off, we would be buried under the timber and no telling how much snow.

We saw our danger as soon as we awoke and John dressed as quickly as he could, took his axe and started for the draw to cut some poles to put under the roof to support it. I was hurrying to get some hot coffee ready for him when he came back, when suddenly there was a frightful crash and I rushed out of the door with Blucher at my heels. The wind was freezing cold and the fine snow filled my mouth and eyes. I tried to call but I could not make myself heard any distance against the roar of the wind. I had nothing on my head and my thin house sweater was very little protection against this bitter cold. I went to the barn but the drift was so high in front of the door that I could not get in there. I was running toward the hill in front of the house shrieking at the top of my lungs when John came up from the other side directly in front of me, dragging a pole under either arm. We went down into the house and put the poles under the roof. The crash had been caused by two of the roof boards cracking from the weight of snow. John brought several poles and braced the roof until he said it was perfectly safe, but I was too frightened to be convinced and begged him to take me to the neighbors.

We knew that we would have to walk for the drift was so deep in front of the barn that we could not get the horses out. Accordingly, we bundled up, much as Anne and I had done in the other blizzard only John and I tied cheese cloth over our faces to keep the fine snow out of our eyes. This proved to be a terrible mistake for we had only gone a short distance when the cheese cloth, damp from our warm breath, became caked with snow and ice and we could not see at all, so we took it off and found our way back to the shelter of the barn. John finally made me understand that we must go back into the house or we would freeze to death. To me there was very little choice between freezing to death and being buried alive, but I finally went with him back into the house. There was no need to struggle any more, so we resigned ourselves to the fate of being buried under the snow once more.

Several hours later we heard a strange noise on the roof of the house and what sounded like a man's voice shouted, "Hello! Hello! Are you there?" John said "Yes, we are here. Who are you and what do you want?" The voice kept calling, "Hello! Hello! Are you there? We are coming! Don't be afraid, we'll soon get you out!"

The scrape, scrape of shovels told us some one was coming to our rescue. In an incredible short time the door opened and in came our homestead neighbor, Mr. Wilson and his two brothers-in-law. They had taken turns at shoveling the snow away from the door for

John's voice had sounded so faint and far way that they expected to find us practically dead from suffocation.

To their surprise, we were not only alive, but seated at the table by the lighted lamp where we had been taking turns reading aloud to each other. What a hearty laugh we all had at the poles under the roof, enough they said, to hold up a skyscraper.

They had grown impatient at the long cold winter and had decided to come and try once more to put up the shack on Mr. Wilson's homestead. They thought the three of them could finish it in a day and then it would be ready to move into as soon as it was warm enough to bring the family over. They had come over the night before in a covered wagon just a short time before the storm struck. They were sleeping in the wagon but as the wind blew so hard during the night, they were afraid it would blow the wagon over. They got out and took the wagon box off of the running gears and put it on the ground. Still they could not sleep for fear that the box would blow away.

The storm had been so fierce all day that they were afraid to start out for our house but as soon as it abated toward evening, they came over to where they thought the house should be, but they could not see any signs of habitation. They were wondering what could have become of us when they saw the smoke coming out of the snow drift. Then they realized what had happened and acted accordingly.

Just a tiny bit of the stovepipe, was protruding above the drift and that gave Mr. Wilson his direction so that he knew where to dig in the drift to find the door. They stayed for a day or two, but as the weather continued so cold that they could not work on the shack, they decided to go back to the Bad Lands and come again later when the severe cold weather was over.

A very kindly rancher used to stop and chat with us every few days. He had a cattle camp on North Fork and the ranch on South Fork of Bad River. Our homestead was about half way between them. He came one day and said that he and his wife would like to have us come over to the ranch February 8 and spend the day with them. I had not been off the place since Christmas day and the proposed trip seemed quite an undertaking for me, but we went.

It was a most delightful experience. The pleasant conversation and exceptionally good food made the day pass so very quickly that our friends insisted that we should not go home, but remain over night and spend the evening playing cards. We played so late that it seemed to me I had not been asleep yet when John asked me to hurry and dress so that we could start home. A morning wind had come up and the snow was melting so fast that we might have trouble in getting across the draws.

He had been up for sometime and had the team already harnessed so that we were able to get started in a short time. We were off none too soon for the snow melted very rapidly and before we reached home the water in some of the draws was quite deep. A nice surprise awaited us on our arrival for our new cow presented us with a baby calf.

The wind kept up all day. About three o'clock in the afternoon we heard a terrible roaring noise. We rushed out on top of the hill to see what it was all about, when we saw a large volume of water coming down Meyer's draw. It soon turned that harmless little stream into a roaring torrent.

While we were watching from the hill, we saw a wagon load of people coming toward our house from the southwest. They reached the house almost as soon as we did and were very much disturbed when they saw that it would be impossible for them to cross the draw that night.

There were six men and three women in the party. They insisted that we should keep them over night so that they could get an early start the next morning. I wished more than ever that our dug out had rubber sides so that I could stretch it to meet these unusual needs. Since it was not, we simply made the best of our crowded conditions and said, "always room for one more."

They were up and away in the early morning but they did not neglect to pay us liberally for our trouble. This shocked my sense of hospitality, but there was no use to try to argue the matter with them for they put the money on the breakfast table and hurried away.

Frankly, we needed the money. All the unusual amount of company that we were having, together with having to feed our stock so much grain, was making great inroads on our very limited capital.

We were happy, indeed, when a railroad contractor rode up to our door on Washington's birthday and offered John a job as cook at a railroad camp about ten miles away.

Oh, I have forgotten to tell you, Sara, that the school board of the Philip District has employed me to teach the spring term of school. This is to start late in March and we thought if John would work at the railroad camp until my school started, that would take care of our finances then he could work on the homestead.

It took John several days to get provisions for the house, feed and hay for the horses and sufficient wood to last me for at least six weeks. A couple of days before John was ready to leave, Mr. Wilson and his brother-in-law arrived from the Bad Lands to begin work on

A school house much like the one Tully would be teaching at.
(Photo courtesy of Earl Knight,
First Half Century, Philip, South Dakota)

Mr. Wilson's shack. The weather was favorable this time and the morning John left they took their belongings up to their shack and I was left alone with my dog.

Mr. Arnet had very kindly offered to take John down to the camp provided he could take our team and wagon so that he could bring some provisions home for his family. This seemed to be a very pleasant arrangement, but if we had not been so grossly ignorant about the care of stock, we would have known that our horses were too weak to undertake this trip.

I expected Mr. Arnet back by noon, but the afternoon wore away and it was about seven o'clock in the evening when I heard him drive up into the yard. In answer to my anxious inquiries, he said, "I have brought you home a dead horse. Well, she 'aint dead yet, but she will be by mornin'. I had to ford streams eleven times, and she took a chill and I thought I was never going to get here."

He helped me unhitch the team and put them in the barn saying that he would bring his own team down and get his provisions in the morning. "Hope your horse don't die tonight." He was off. I was alone with my little dog, no one to help me, and a desperately sick horse to care for.

She lay in her stall and shook as though she were having a chill. I knew absolutely nothing about the care of a well horse to say nothing of a sick animal. I put both horse blankets over her, and remembering my experience with my sick dog, I put the hot water bottle across the small of her back. Then I made some very thin gruel out of cream of wheat which I gave her out of a bottle. After she had the warm gruel she stopped shaking and got up on her feet. I strapped a horse blanket on her, left plenty of hay and grain where she could reach it and went to bed. She was still standing up when I went down to see about her in the middle of the night, but the next morning when I went to the barn, she was down with her head caught under the bottom board on the calf pen that we had built in there.

I was able to break the board loose with the axe, but I could not get the horse up. She looked at me so pitifully that I ran almost all the way up to Arnet's to ask him to please come right away and help me. He said, "there is no use to get so excited about it for the horse will die anyway, but if it will make you feel any better, I will come down after I have my breakfast and see what we can do for her." I ran almost all the way back home only to find her standing up in her own stall. I gave her a drink of water, then went in to get my breakfast. I was surely tired and hungry.

Soon after I had finished eating, Mr. Arnet rode up and said, "I see your horse is standing up. I am glad of that for I don't know what to do for her. In fact, I don't think anyone can do anything for her. She can't possibly live, and is too far gone now for help so you may just as well make up your mind to that."

I thanked him for coming and stood and watched him as he rode out of sight over the hill. Then I went back to the barn to take a look at the horse, and I found her down in the stall once more.

It seemed a pity to let the pretty thing lie there and die without making an effort to save her, so I thought I would go for Mr. Wilson this time. Maybe he knew more about horses than Mr. Arnet. It was worth trying.

I bundled up as best I could for by this time it was snowing very hard from the east. Since I had to wade across the draw I wrapped my feet in newspaper and then pulled on my rubber boots. The water was much deeper than I thought, for it ran over the tops of my boots and got my feet wet, but, I thought I could keep warm walking.

This was my first trip to the Wilson shack but I had heard the men say that you could see it from the road after you went between two hills which we always called, "The Pass." Sure enough, when I went through The Pass there was the shack in the distance and the road seemed to lead directly to it.

The storm had grown worse since I left home and the snow beating into my face made it so difficult to see that I put my head down and followed along in the wagon track. After some little time, I came up to not one building, but three buildings, two homestead shacks and a barn.

I knew then that I had followed an old hay road and gone southeast instead of northeast. There was no one at home in either shack, so I rested a few minutes at the barn and then started in the direction of Wilson's shack. At least, I thought I did, but very soon, I was back at the three buildings once more. I made several attempts to get my bearings and get away from these buildings but each time I would come back.

By this time, I realized that I was so lost I tried to break into one of the shacks. There was not a stick or a stone to be found and my bare hands were so stiff and cold that they were useless. I gave up then and started for home, but by this time the snow had obliterated my tracks and in a few minutes, I found myself back at the three buildings. Then I was thoroughly frightened. I put my arms around my dog's neck and asked "Blucher, can you find home? I can't!"

He ran a little way from me in what I thought was the opposite direction from our house. He sat down and waited. The thought came to me, "Well, maybe he knows what he is doing. Surely I don't." Accordingly I followed him. He would run ahead a little ways and then wait for me to catch up. He did this until we came to "The Pass." Then I knew where I was and was able to go the rest of the way rather quickly. There I found the older Arnet boy waiting for me. He had ridden over on horse back. His mother had sent him down to see if he could be of any help.

When he found that I had been lost trying to get Mr. Wilson to come and help me, he offered to ride over there and ask him to come. It was growing bitterly cold by this time, and I was hungry and chilled through.

After starting the fire I took off my boots and frozen stockings and a great deal of the skin from my poor frost bitten heels and toes. They had been frosted so many times the skin was like tissue paper.

Mr. Wilson left his work and came down immediately. He was such a comfort. He went out and looked at the horse, then came in and said, "Your horse is not going to die, I have seen much sicker animals than she is get well. Make me about two quarts of hot pumpkin seed tea."

We gave her the tea. He sat up with her almost all night. I do not know what else he did for her, but when I went down to the barn early the next morning, she was standing up in her stall eating her grain. "A friend in need is a friend indeed." Thank God for good neighbors.

My poor feet are swollen so badly this morning that I am hobbling around in John's shoes. I can't even get my bed room slippers on.

Mr. Wilson is going over to the Bad Lands and get his family and they will live here in our house and take care of things, and I shall go and stay with Mother and Anne until my feet get better.

I shall mail this as I go through Philip.

Much love to you all.

Tully

Difficulties Ahead

March 12, 1907

Dear Cousin Sara:

It really was quite an experience to make the trip over to Mother's. Mr. Wilson and his family got to our house just at dark on Thursday evening. My feet were in such terrible condition that they insisted that I should start very early the next morning so that Mother could take care of them as soon as possible. Mrs. Wilson was afraid I would have blood poisoning in them.

Mr. Wilson took me over to Mr. Cook's place which was a homestead shack near the road that was travelled by practically all the teamsters who freighted for the railroad construction camps. John had stopped at Cook's on his trips for provisions. Mrs. Cook and the children were homesick for Iowa. When John told them about me they insisted that he should bring me with him next time, so I was very happy to stop at their place.

There are many teams making this trip now, for the railroad company, the Pierre and Rapid City, is putting forth strenuous effort to get this railroad built so that they can get the benefit of this influx of settlers into this newly opened country lying west of the Missouri river between Pierre and Rapid City.

Mr. Wilson went on to the camp where John was working to get some more grain for the horses, and it just happened that two men who were neighbors of my brother had just brought a big load of grain up to that camp from Midland. They told John and Mr. Wilson that they would be glad to stop for me and would take me to Mother's, but that it would be very late when they were ready to start. I was still so much afraid of riding in a wagon that it was quite a relief to know that I was not going to be obliged to take the trip with entire strangers.

This day of waiting seemed very long indeed for the men did not come until almost dark and it had begun to drizzle rain when they got here. They made me as comfortable as they could in the back of the wagon among the horse blankets. My little dog snuggled down with me under my umbrella and we were off for a long, tedious ride. When we got to the place where we should have turned into my Mother's place, it was so dark that we could not see the gate. It was raining so hard I did not want them to bother for me and I said I would go on to the ranch where they were going as the people there kept a road house.

It was almost midnight when we got there and I shall never forget the kindness of that lovely woman. As soon as she found out who I was and why I had come, she did everything she could to make me comfortable. She knew Mother very well and I think she tried to take her place that night for she insisted upon getting me a warm supper and then had me share her own daughter's room.

She told me that I did not need to worry about getting back to my Mother's place in the morning for she would see to it that I got a ride back. In fact, she said "Big Steve" was going out early in the morning with a six-horse load of grain and she would arrange for me to ride with him.

I was so tired that it seemed to me that I had only fallen asleep when she came and wakened me very quickly and said "Steve" would be starting in half an hour. I was dressed and ready to go in a few minutes, but with some foreboding, I'll admit, for it was just pouring. "Big Steve" helped me up on to the bags of grain and gave a hearty "haw! haw!" when my dog scrambled up beside me.

We had not gone very far when we came to a steep hill. The earth was terribly rutted from the heavy hauling over it and we had only gone a short distance on the climb until we were stuck. The big horses pulled and strained and "Big Steve" urged them with all the swear words that could be included in a teamster's vocabulary, I think. He would say occasionally, "Excuse me lady, but these horses are used to this kind of language."

How he laughed when I offered to get down so as to make the load lighter. He said, "Why you're such a mite these horses don't even know you are there."

Soon another wagon load of grain pulled up behind us. The teamsters took horses from that load and hitched them on ahead of our lead team and we were soon up the hill, but we waited until our horses had helped the other load up hill before we started slowly creeping along the muddy road. The creaking of the load and the straining of the harness was music in my ears, for it meant that we were nearer to our destination.

"Big Steve" helped me down at my mother's gate, and I felt that I had made a breach of etiquette when I offered to pay for he looked down at me in a kindly sort of way and said, "Lady, we all just don't take money for ginin' a friendly lift to a body."

Mother and Anne did not see us coming. Anne opened the door in answer to my knock. She gave one little shriek of delight, then said, "Oh mother, come and see who is here. They look like two downed rats!" Such was my welcome home.

It was such a joy to be with them. I think I had been very heart hungry to see mother and did not realize what the matter was with me. Mother knew just what to do for my feet. She made me stay in bed for a day or two and by that time they were so much better that I could get around very well, and we spent the rest of the week in having a grand good time.

Anne and I had been over to brother Sam's one day and as we were coming home about dusk, I saw a man walking towards us. I said, "Why that is John. Something must be wrong or he would not be here." "John nothing" said Miss Anne. "You surely have a vivid imagination. You want it to be John, so you think it is." But I was right. It was John and I knew when I looked into his eyes that he had a message for me. He said in a very casual way, "When I got the mail yesterday there was this letter for you which I knew you would want very much. The camp where I have been working has finished the work here. They are going to move out toward Rapid City. I quit yesterday so that I could bring this letter over to you today."

We were nearing Anne's shack now and imagine my delight when I saw our own team tied to the wagon and eating grain. My sick horse was well again and was really getting fat. I hurried into the light to see what the mysterious letter was about. I found that it was from the County Superintendent of Schools telling me that it would be necessary for me to come into Fort Pierre to take the teacher's examination which was to be held Friday and Saturday of that week.

She went on to explain that she had told me previously that she would endorse my certificate from Nebraska, but that there were some teachers in the community of Philip who held certificates in South Dakota, so that she had reconsidered and it would now be necessary for me to come to Fort Pierre and take the regular teachers' examination. This was like a blow between the eyes, for it was Wednesday evening. Fort Pierre was seventy miles away. Our horses were not able to make such a long trip and I could not formulate any workable plans for such a trip in some little time.

We finally decided that John and Anne should take me down to Midland about thirty miles away and that I could go on the train the rest of the way. We hoped that it would get to Fort Pierre by Friday but there was really no assurance that it would make that good time.

We had only been on the road about an hour the next morning when a man and his son overtook us. They knew Anne very well and reined their horses up by our wagon for a chat. Anne told them where we were going and why. They asked me to ride on to Midland with them. This pleased us very much. John helped me into their wagon and he went back with Anne to Mother's to wait for me. The train was late in leaving Midland and did not reach Fort Pierre until almost morning, so I just had a nap before I went to the court house for my examinations. They were not too difficult and I was the happy possessor of a first grade certificate in South Dakota before time for my school to start.

There was no train back to Midland after I finished my examinations on Saturday so that it was necessary for me to stay in Fort Pierre until Monday. This proved to be a very pleasant experience for me for on Sunday morning the editor of the Fair Play, Mr. Mix and his wife came to call on me. Mr. Mix and I were both born in the little town of Smith Center, Kansas and had spent our early childhood there. It was great fun reminiscing about the people we had known there. When I mentioned that I was going as far as Midland on the train the next morning, Mr. Mix said, "Here is where we declare a holiday for ourselves and go with you. I have always had a desire to see that "west river" country. They tell me that the grass is so short out there that they put baskets over the noses of the calves at weaning time for they are so much more nimble than the cows that they run ahead and eat up all the feed." I surely liked his humorous side light on why we muzzled calves but I liked much more the prospect of their very pleasant company on the trip out.

We reached Midland just about noon. There was a stage, four horse, apparently ready to start, standing in front of one of the eating houses. We asked the driver if he would wait for us to go over to the hotel and get dinner. He said, "Yes, if you are here at one o'clock, we leave just on time."

We hurried through our dinner and got back to where we had left the stage at about five minutes of one, but we could not see the stage. Mr. Mix made inquiry here and there until we found a man who said, "Oh, you're lookin' for the stage. Why that feller got a load and left here about ten minutes ago. He said if a woman comes here to see about goin' on the stage, tell her we had a load and I thought she could catch a ride up some other way."

Gus Stoermer's stage brought many of the homesteaders
to Philip from Midland where the railroad ended.
He operated his stage mostly on Bad River and from Midland
to Philip. (Photo courtesy of Mrs. M. B. Poste,
First Half Century, Philip, South Dakota*)*

This was disconcerting to say the least. I was hopeless for I did not know any of these people or where they came from or where they were going, but Mr. Mix was equal to the occasion. He found a freighter who was leaving town soon with a load of grain to be delivered at a railroad camp about three miles from Mother's.

This part of the trip was uneventful. The mules were slow but they were able to pull the load through all the mud holes and we reached the railroad camp just at dusk. I followed the railroad grade as it ran very near Anne's shack. I was not afraid of getting lost but

I had not taken the railroad bridges into consideration and when I came to the first one I got so dizzy I very nearly fell, but I did not intend this handicap to be my undoing, so I got down on my hands and knees and crawled across. This would not have been quite so difficult if I had been willing to part with a large bundle of magazines that the Mix friends had given me. At times I was tempted to throw them away but I was so eager for something new to read that I carried them on. They were so heavy that I had to rest often.

It was very late when I reached Anne's shack and every one had gone to bed. John had gone up to Mother's shack and taken my dog with him. When the dog heard my voice, he came as fast as he could, making little barks of joy. The family seemed very happy, but I think the dog was more pleased than any of them to see me, at least he gave more expression to his emotion.

John and I got over to our own home about dark the next evening. The Wilsons seemed very happy to see us. I felt that "Stay, stay at home, dear heart, and rest. Home keeping hearts are happiest," must have been written just for me. It was so good to be back in our home, although our home was only a sod dug out.

The homing instinct seems so strong in me, I wonder sometimes if I am normal in my thinking.

It does not seem that an intelligent woman capable of making a good living anywhere would be willing to go through with all these experiences just for a humble little place that we can call our own home.

Truly, "Home is where the heart is."

> Much love to you.
> Tully

The Country School

April 29, 1907

Dear Cousin Sara:

There were only two weeks left before the opening of school, and as we bid the Wilsons God speed when they left for their own home, we went back into the house to formulate our plans as there was much to be done about the place before I went away to teach.

We had considered the advisability of my driving back and forth from school, but a ten mile trip every day and five barbed wire gates to open and close seemed to much of an undertaking. Accordingly, we made a trip down to the homestead shack that we had seen as we came up from crossing the North Fork of Bad River on our first trip out to the homestead. It was a delight to find the white haired woman, Mrs. Arthur, just as charming as I had imagined she would be from the glimpse that I had caught of her from the covered wagon.

She hesitated for a long time about taking a stranger into their crowded quarters, but after much persuasion on my part, she said that I might come for a week and perhaps by that time we could tell if the arrangement would be pleasant for all concerned.

I feel that her decision has given me a true friend whom I hope to keep through out my life for I not only spent three very happy

71 ~

months with the Arthur's, but their close friendship has been a constant source of joy to me.

Since this arrangement would necessitate my being away from home from Monday morning until Friday night of each week, we sent for my sister June and her husband Paul to come on right away and live at our house while they were putting up their shack and getting ready to establish residence on their own land. As they were young and eager for adventure, our plans suited them perfectly. They did not even wait for a return message from us so that they arrived almost as soon as their letter did, telling us that they were coming right away.

I was busy on Sunday morning after their arrival getting things packed ready to start school the next morning when a buggy drove up and two very charming women got out and came to the door. Their faces showed so much animation that I knew they were not merely coming to call, but had come on some special errand. I invited them into the house and did not have to wait long to learn their mission, for as soon as the conventional pleasantries had been passed, they asked John if he would be interested in going into business in the new town of Philip when it was moved to the new town site as it would be when the railroad was completed as far as Philip. They thought that perhaps by the middle of April or the first of May that things would be opening up in the new town.

John assured them that he had no desire to leave the homestead for he was planning on planting out a crop of corn which he hoped would yield enough to enable him to feed some hogs and some milk cows. In this way he could get a foot hold in the farming game which he felt was the ideal life for a family man. Our guests, however, were not so easily put off. They were close friends of Aunt Louise and her family in Sioux City, Iowa and through them they heard that John was an experienced baker and restaurant man.

The discussion lasted throughout the forenoon. Many plans were proposed and talked over. They really wanted to start a restaurant, or lunch counter, with a bakery in connection. They were willing to put up the capital against John's labor and form a partnership on that basis.

I really felt sorry for John for it was very difficult for him to decide what to do. He had dreamed for a long time of having a home on a farm where he could be his own "lord and master." On the other hand, our finances were at such a very low ebb that if he undertook farming right then it would be necessary for me to assume the responsibility of furnishing the bread and butter money for several months at least.

Farming in a new country was such an uncertain venture. If we were unfortunate enough to have a drought or hot winds, we would have a crop failure, no matter how much labor he would expend on the farm. A business venture in a new town was also most uncertain. Perhaps the new town would not develop into anything more than a trading post.

The prospect of a partnership business that might end in failure made no appeal to John. Then our new found friends made him a proposition to be a baker for them and let them assume all the responsibility for the business, and pay him a salary. This last proposition was finally agreed upon and John was to go to work for them on May first.

Our guests left for home in the late afternoon and John and I sat down to talk things over, for our plans of the morning had been so changed that we were at a loss to know what we should do to make this new adjustment.

Of course there was a possibility that Paul would consider putting in some crop for us. We were obliged to put in five acres of crop in order that we might prove up on our land in the fall. It seemed to me that this would be the best arrangement for I had the assurance that I could have my position back in the Wakefield high school if I cared for it for the next school year.

When John gave his promise to go to work in Philip on May first, I knew that he would do it for he took great pride in keeping a promise, but I must say that he was torn with indecision all during the day Monday and Tuesday following our decided change of plans. He would say sometimes, "I think I shall just ride over to Hay Draw and tell those people that I have changed my mind and that I want to farm my own land. No, I can't do that, for I have given my word to go to work for them on May first."

We did not accomplish any work that day for we would just get nicely started at something when some incident would bring up the subject of our change of plans and then we would stop for another long discussion.

Perhaps it was best for all concerned that June and Paul arrived very unexpectedly on Tuesday afternoon. Bill Smith had gone into Philip for the mail. He was much surprised when the stage came in from Murdo to find that June and Paul were among the passengers. He brought them right on out with him and thoroughly enjoyed watching us be surprised.

Paul was delighted with the prospect of working for us so that he could get the use of our team to make the necessary improvements on his land. Things moved fast from that time on until I was ready to start for school on March 15th.

John and I drove down to Mr. Arthur's in the afternoon. We did not talk at all until their little homestead shack was in sight then John said, "So this is where you will be, and I shall be in town. This is a far cry from what we have planned, 'a home of our own.'"

Maybe I haven't pioneer courage, but at any rate, I tried to be brave and said, "It takes money to buy plows, harrows and seed for planting. We are not abandoning our plans, we are only delaying their execution. We will work and save our money and perhaps by next year we can farm."

Mrs. Arthur was so charming when we stopped at the house to leave my luggage that I felt if our trial week of living together did not prove satisfactory that it would be my fault, and not hers.

Since my school books and supplies were heavy, John said he would drive on over to the school house and leave them there. I went with him for I had a great curiosity to see what a log school house would be like inside. The building was about sixteen feet square with the walls made of rough logs while the ceiling was made of hewn logs and poles. A big hewn log made the ridge pole down the center of the ceiling. It rested on a pole in the center of the room and one at either end of the room. A similar hewn log was placed under each of the eaves. This made the frame work for the poles in the ceiling, or roof. These poles, when covered with a generous coating of dirt, made a very satisfactoy roof. There were two windows on either side of the room with a big heavy door squarely in the center of the south end of the building. A black board ran across the north end of the room.

The two-room school house in Philip, built in 1907.
It was abandoned when the brick school was built in 1910 but used
again after the fire of 1914. (Photo courtesy of Mrs. Fred Haberly,
First Half Century, Philip, South Dakota)

When John tried to open the heavy door, we found that one hinge was broken so that the door had to be lifted. The plank floor was warped until the door would only open about half way. A large box wood stove stood in the center of the room. It was badly cracked and the ashes had sifted out on to the floor. There were several home made desks on either side of the room with a kitchen table up in front for a teacher's desk.

In spite of the fact that there seemed to be plenty of "chinking" between the logs, the dust had blown in badly and the field mice had scattered the floor with weed seeds. John swept out and helped me put my materials in place. He suggested that I have the children bring some tin cans from home which I could unsolder and nail over the holes in the floor to keep the mice out.

I really think he was not thinking so much about the mice as he was about the danger from rattle snakes, for the school house was very near a prairie dog town. We had been told that there were always many rattle snakes in these dog towns.

By the time we had the building arranged to my satisfaction, it was nearing sun down so I insisted that John go directly home and let me walk back to Mr. Arthur's. As I went into the yard at the Arthurs', I looked toward the west in time to see John in the wagon silhouetted against the sky just before he disappeared over the hill. He seemed to be going "On, on into the sunset."

The next morning found me at the school house bright and early, eager for this new adventure of pioneer school teaching. I did not have long to wait for the children began to arrive about eight o'clock, most of them came on horse back from the nearby ranches. But three little girls drove a single horse hitched to a two wheeled cart. They came from a ranch about four miles away on the North Fork of Bad River.

Mr. Jenkins who keeps the store at Philip is clerk of the district. He brought his two children this first morning so that he could tell me to admit as many children from the railroad camps as I could accommodate in the school room. A carpenter at one of the camps had volunteered to make the necessary desks for them. It seemed a shame to refuse to let any child come to school in that out-of-the-way place, so I found when I took the roll the first morning that I had twenty-six children enrolled with all eight grades represented.

They were an interesting group and sometimes taxed my ingenuity to the limit.

I had been warned that "Big Bill" was the bad boy of that country and that he had made serious trouble for every teacher who had ever taught there.

One morning not long after the term opened, several of the small children came rushing into the school house screaming like wild Indians. They said "Big Bill has a lot of porcupine quills that he is shooting at us. He says he will put our eyes out." I called Bill and he came slouching into the room with a look on his face that said, "Well, what are you going to do about it?"

He seemed a bit non plussed when I said, "Bill, the children say you have some porcupine quills. You know I have never seen a porcupine or even a porcupine quill. Would you mind letting me see some of those that you have?" He took several from his pocket and I said, "Oh, you have several. About how many quills does a porcupine have?" He seemed quite pleased to show me that he had many quills. He searched in his pocket and found all of them. We had quite a collection which we put in a match box to show at our nature study lesson that morning.

We began to search the dictionary, our readers, nature study books, and all the other books that we thought would tell us about porcupines so that we could have a lesson about them. Big Bill told for his part of the lesson how his dog had caught this particular porcupine and had gotten ever so many quills in his nose and mouth. Bill had used the pliers and pulled out as many quills as he could reach but the poor dog would probably suffer terribly for some time from some of the quills that he could not get out. Bill had found his dog was fighting with a porcupine; he ran to the house and brought his gun and soon killed his dog's enemy. The children were thrilled with his story and Bill became the hero of the day.

This proved to be a very happy incident so far as the school was concerned, for Bill tried to retain his reputation as a student of nature. So it was Bill who brought us the first pussy willow, the first snow drops, the Johnny jump ups, and so on. Then he assumed the role of 'man-around-the-house' and cut as much wood as he could from the old blocks and stumps that were piled in the front yard for stove wood.

The pack rats and mice became very annoying. They would carry the crayon and small pencils to their nests back of the ridge poles. Bill conceived the idea of coming early in the mornings and poking these nests out on the floor and rescuing the plunder. Every once in awhile when I would get to school, I would find Bill hard at work poking these nests out on the floor. Or perhaps, he would have finished his work but would leave the nests on the floor until I would get there so that I could see them; then he would sweep the floor and wait for the children to come so that he could tell what he had found during that raid.

He seemed so proud of himself that I never dared to tell that so far as I was concerned, I had never been able to decide which struck more terror in my soul—a mouse or a rattle snake.

I told you, Sara, that most of the children came on horse back. No doubt you have been wondering what we did with all those saddle horses all day long. In this western country, it seems to be a very simple matter to take care of a horse. Each child brings a long rope that he calls a lariat. They tie one end of it to the horse's halter

Philip students on their way to school.
(Photo courtesy Mrs. T. G. Thorson, Haaken Horizons)

while the other end is fastened to a long iron pin with a swivel in the top of it so the rope will not wind around the pin as the horse roams about eating. This arrangement is fine unless some horse gets tangled up in his lariat rope. If the rope gets fastened around his foot he will pull until he burns the back of his foot. When any child sees his horse struggling in a tangled lariat rope, he dashes wildly from the school room to help his precious mount extricate himself.

When I was planning my work before school opened, I wondered what these children would be interested in for playground activities. This need not have concerned me very much for they are interested in games quite new to me.

They stage Indian fights which are unique in the way they work out in detail, but when they are not so blood thirsty they go out in to the prairie dog town and snare stoats. They make a loop in a long piece of cord. After placing this loop around the rim of a prairie dog hole, they lie down flat on their stomachs in a circle around the hole. They keep perfectly quiet until some luckless stoat puts his head up out of the hole, when they jerk the string quickly, drawing up the loop tightly around the neck of the stoat. They say that the stoats are a menace to the ranchers' poultry, so they feel that they are good citizens by helping to rid the country of the pests. The four smallest children are not interested in snaring stoats and the older children are not particularly interested in having them join the circle, for it is too hard to keep the little folks from talking or making some kind of noise; but they too are resourceful in finding amusement. One little girl who had Indian blood in her veins, lives on a ranch over on the South Fork of Bad River and rides a gentle black horse to school. She takes three of the other children on the horse with her and they ride up and down the road in front of the school house until I ring the bell. Then they ride up where I can see them, and each in turn slides down over the horse's tail. The first time that I saw this performance, it alarmed me somewhat for fear that the horse would object to this unusual procedure and remonstrate with his heels. He seemed to enjoy the fun as much as the kiddies and this has grown to be a daily affair.

Soon after school started the County Superintendent of schools sent word to me that there would be a Teachers and Officers' meeting held in our school house on Friday, April 11th. She asked me to prepare a paper for the program and make all necessary arrangements. I sent a notice of this meeting to the clerk of the school district and asked him to post it in the store and I also sent a notice to the post master and asked him to put it up in the post office.

The children entered into the spirit of the affair so that we soon had a program well under way. I asked my good friend, Mrs. Arthur, if she would be kind enough to allow me to bring the county superintendent to her home for lunch.

On the Friday morning of April 11, the children came to school early. Some of them brought beautiful bouquets of flowers. We decorated our school room and put our best school work on display and were ready by ten o'clock to receive our local school officers and the visiting county superintendent. Big Bill who had been in command of the forces at work had stationed our four little folks at the gate to tell us when our guests were coming. Soon after ten they came swooping into the school room shouting, "There are not four people—there are twenty people—fifty people—lots and lots of people!"

I hurried to the door and took a look. The children were partially right at least, for there were ever and ever so many people coming. This was the first public meeting that had been called since the new settlers had come to Philip and so they just closed up shop and came. The little school house could not accomodate all of them but they stayed anyway.

The children gave their part of the program first and I was proud of them. The rest of the program was long, but the audience seemed greatly interested. When the noon hour came, I thought of Mrs. Arthur having an appetizing lunch waiting and suggested that we have an hour of intermission. This suggestion was quickly over ruled and we finished about two o'clock. This was a new experience to me. I had never seen people before who were willing to fore go food to listen to a school program.

When the last person left that afternoon, I hurriedly closed up the school house and went over to Mrs. Arthur's to explain why I had not brought my guest for lunch. She was terribly disappointed to think that she had stayed at home and kept a lunch waiting for people who did not come when she could have been at the school mingling with a crowd of people—a privilege she had been denied for many months. She showed her disappointment in her face, but her son expressed himself in terms that I readily understood. I did not blame any of them for this unusually fine mother was idolized by her husband and her three grown sons. They could not bear to think of her being deprived of anything that would give her pleasure.

Our school has one very bright boy. He is short and rather stout with a sunny disposition and an extremely keen mind. This is his second year in school and he is in the fourth grade.

One day I looked over at him and saw his face covered with confusion. I said, "What is the matter, William?" He said, "I can't do my Arithmetic."

"Bring your tablet here and I will help you find your trouble." He came up to me and handed me his tablet. I said, "I want your pencil." He looked me straight in the eyes and said, "I don't think you do." This answer coming from William was so unexpected that I suppose I assumed a school ma'am voice when I said, "William where is your pencil?"

"If you please, ma'am, it is inside my pants."

The poor child had been rubbing his pencil across his neck when it slipped out of his hand and slid down inside his clothes.

The children who come from the railroad camps had been reporting from time to time the progress that was being made on the railroad. One morning they came in very much excited telling us that the first train was to come into Philip May 9th. Mr. Jenkins, the clerk of the school board, sent word for me to bring all the children down to Philip right after lunch on May 9 so that they might see the first train come into town.

I knew, of course, that this was the right thing to do, but I rather dreaded the responsibility of caring for so many children during all that excitement. I need not have been so concerned for when we reached town all the parents were there. They took the children with them and I was free to enjoy, for the second time in my life, the experience of seeing the first train arrive in a frontier town. Did I ever tell you about it? It was when I was a very small child that I saw the first train come into Smith Center, Kansas and watched Mabel Corn, the first child who had been born in that town, drive the golden spike. Susan Lane and I put crossed pins on the rail road track so that when the train ran over them they would make little scissors. Then we rode in the caboose and the coal car. When we assembled at school the next morning I told the children about these childhood experiences of mine. They were all so thrilled with what they had seen that they could scarcely wait to tell about what they had seen the day before. They all wanted to tell me at the same time.

Little Andrew Jenkins sat very near my desk, so near in fact that when he would give his long curls a toss, one would frequently rest on my books or papers. He gave my skirt a little tug when I looked down at him he said, "If you will give me some paper, some scissors, and some paste, I'll make something for you." I gave him the necessary materials and went on about my work. When I came up to his desk after a little while, I saw he had made the most adorable little paper engine, drive wheels, cab, smoke stack, coal car and all. I placed it on the palm of my hand and held it up for all the children to see saying, "Children, see what a fine engine Andrew has made for us." He looked at it and said, "Oh, please let me have it just a minute." I handed it back to him. He cut a tiny square of paper and pasted it in front of the smoke stack. I said, "Andrew, what is that?" His tone showed that he felt sorry for my ignorance when he said, "Why, that's the head light!"

No doubt, you have gathered before this that I stayed on with Mrs. Arther throughout the term. We made the arrangement at the close of the first week that I should stay with her from Monday morning until Friday night each week.

June and Paul used to come for me on Friday afternoon and bring me back very early on Monday morning. I liked these early morning rides with the snappy air so fresh and fragrant with the growing grasses, but best of all were the meadow larks. They were here, there, and everywhere. Their lovely song could be heard above all the other bird songs of the prairies.

We arrived at the school house one Monday morning long before any of the children came. My mind was so filled with the lovely lark songs that I wrote this little poem.

The Meadow Lark Chorus of the Morning

When the dawn across the prairie steals
The grasses and the green leaves feel
The soft touch of the gentle breeze
As the clear musical call of a meadow lark
Heralds the morning.

The rosy tints light the eastern sky
This beautiful singer soars on high
As his kind near by take up his call
Then the circle is widened till it seems that all
Yellow throated larks have joined
The meadow larks chorus of the morning.

As the breeze grows stronger
New life stirs
Still the volume grows
And no pause occurs
In the meadow lark chorus of the morning.

It seems these lovely creatures
May split their throats
In their wild desire
To sing the notes
Of praise to Him
Who lets wild birds sing
A meadow lark chorus in the morning

As our school term was drawing to a close we began to plan for a picnic for the last day. We made out a program of foot races, potato races, relay races, and many games.

The girls made up a menu and told each child what he should bring. They were so happy anticipating this good time that they could scarcely wait for the day to come. Perhaps it was well that they had so much pleasure in anticipation for just the day before school closed all the children from the railroad camps had to leave. The work on the railroad was finished there and the camps moved on. These children were to have such an important part in the picnic program as it had been planned that the children who were left thought they would rather have the picnic in the school yard and go home early on the last day. It was arranged that way. My first school in South Dakota is over.

I have written you about it at great length, Sara, for it has meant much to me.

Your devoted cousin

Tully

Our First Summer

My dear Sara:

I dreaded for school to close for John had gone to work in the Bakery down town and June and Paul were eager to get into their own home on their own land. Of course, that was quite the natural thing for them to do, but their shack was at least a quarter of a mile from our house across Meyers' draw.

That meant that Blucher and I must live on the homestead by ourselves, for houses were not available in Philip. Even if such an arrangement could have been made, John would never have consented to it for he was very sure that he would soon be back to farm our own homestead.

The ranchers kept trying to discourage him from making plans for farming. They told him that this was a ranch country and not a farming country on account of the irregularity of the rainfall. They said that sometimes we would have an abundance of rain but that it would not come at the right time to produce crops. Their advice to him was not to put much money in farm machinery but to buy cattle, possibly calves at weaning time. In this way he could build up a herd without much capital, for they were sure that a cattle ranch would be a much better bet than a "dry farm."

Street scene of Philip's first
Harvest Festival, September 1907.
(Haaken Horizons)

No one seemed able to convince John, for the heavy snow of the winter taken with an abundance of spring rain made the grass grow luxuriantly everywhere, especially on the low land and along the draws. This was proof enough for John that crops would grow here. He said, "Of course we will have dry years. Every farming country has its droughts or dry years." He seemed to have the desire, prompted more by sentiment than reason, that he break the sod for our first field that we were planning to plant to sod corn. It was impossible for him to get away from the bakery to do this so we hired our neighbor on the south to plow the field and plant the corn, also to plow a garden patch for me. He plowed the garden on Saturday so that I could drop the potato cuttings in the furrows and the next time round the freshly turned sod would cover them. I had planned for this garden long before we left Nebraska and had brought with me an abundance of all the different kinds of garden seeds that I thought would grow in virgin soil. Mother told me that root vegetables would do better than vegetables that bear fruit above the ground. I am sure that she had proven this by her experience in Kansas, so I planted a large patch of radishes, turnips, rutabagas, carrots, parsnips and onions. There was still a chance that other things might do well so I put in peas, beans, cucumbers, water melons and musk melons, and set out about three dozen tomato plants that I had raised in the house. This garden was my joy and delight, but when it was finished, I knew that I had let my enthusiasm run away with my judgment. I realized this more and more, for as the heavy warm rains brought up the young vegetables, they also brought up an ever increasing crop of weeds.

I had not counted on this for there were no weeds in the prairie grasses so why should there be weeds in my garden. Where did they come from anyway? I did not have time to search for an answer to that question for I was kept busy trying to keep them cut down so that they would not choke out my young vegetables.

Every morning, as soon as it was light, I would get up and get my breakfast and then take Blucher and my hoe and go to the garden and hoe weeds until the sun would get so hot that I would have to go back to the house.

When John came home for the week ends he would help with the hoeing, but I think he really helped more by praising my efforts for then I would work harder than ever the next week.

I talked to him very seriously about putting a fence around my garden. He assured me again and again that that was a waste of money for the ranchers had all put their stock in pastures for the summer so there was no danger of trespass, and we could ill afford a fence since we would have to hire it built as well as furnish the materials.

I was silenced but not convinced for my garden had become the absorbing interest of my life and since there was nothing else to take its place, I was very grateful for it. It seemed so satisfying for I had more radishes, onions, carrots and turnips than I could use, and it gave me great pleasure to send sacks of these fresh vegetables to my neighbors who did not have gardens. There was one terrible draw back to this garden work and that was the mosquitoes. They came in perfect swarms. I wore stockings on my arms and a piece of mosquito netting over my sunbonnet. I brought the mosquito netting down under my dress neck so that the pests could not crawl under it. Of course they out witted me very often.

The men wore mosquito netting over their hats to protect their faces and necks, and they also fastened strips of cloth to the bridles of the horses so that as the horse moved his head in walking, these strips would shoo the flies and mosquitoes away from the horse's nostrils as they worked.

One night about the middle of July Blucher got up out of his bed and came over by my bed and he gave a low growl. I could see by the moon light that came in through the window that the hair was standing up straight between his shoulders.

Of course I thought that there was some one prowling about the premises and I was so frightened that I lay there cold and rigid.

Blucher walked back and forth growling for a moment or two and then gave one spring out through the mosquito netting that covered the east window and he was gone into the night.

Things seemed even worse to me then for I had the added fear that something might happen to him. I did not have long to wait until I heard his pitiful whining at the door. I opened it and there he stood, the poor thing. The skin was torn in many places across his chest and on his legs. He was bleeding badly.

I no longer feared for myself but for him. I built a fire quickly and was soon able to bathe his cuts with hot Lysol water. I bandaged up his legs and made a jacket for him of a piece of an old sheet that I had for I thought that the flies and mosquitoes would torture him otherwise.

It was so nearly time to get up when I had all this done that I got our breakfast thinking that I would have a long time to work in the garden before it got hot.

I took my hoe and started for the garden, but I told Blucher that he had better stay in the house where he would be cool. He seemed to feel differently about it and came limping along at my heels whining at every step until I picked him up and carried him.

When we got to the top of the little hill overlooking the garden, I realized what it was all about, for my beautiful garden was completely wrecked. The cattle had broken out of the pasture near by and had eaten what they wanted in the garden and trampled the rest into the ground. It was a complete loss.

I sat down with my dog in my lap, put my arms around his neck and cried as if my heart would break.

Blucher's wounds would not submit to so much affectionate hugging, so that he wiggled loose from my arms and sat close beside me whining. All at once he pointed his nose up in the air and gave a most piteous wail. My sense of humor at the ridiculous picture we made sitting here came to my rescue and I got up and went back to the house to formulate new plans.

Up to this time I had not thought of our field of sod corn on the flat above the house so I went up there to see if the cattle had destroyed that. Thanks to Blucher, it was all right. They had not even been in the field. But I did find that the sun flowers were getting quite a start.

I turned to Blucher and said, "Thanks old man, for your quick work this morning. This field seems to need attention, however, so we shall turn our energy here."

When John came home that week end, although he found that the garden was utterly destroyed, he also had the pleasure of seeing that many rows of corn had been freed from weeds. Since he also felt quite conscience stricken to think that he had refused to fence my garden, he went to one of the neighbors and made arrangements to have a fence put around our corn field.

John thought that it was necessary for him to go back to work this week on Sunday afternoon. I did not want him to go so early, but as he insisted I walked with him for a couple of miles. There was a tree near one of the draws which we had to cross. I took a book with me and sat under this tree and read until the wind sprang up and I knew I must be going if I got home before dark.

I had worn a light dress with a very full skirt and as the wind was blowing quite hard by the time I reached the top of the hill just before we went through The Pass, my skirt would blow out so far and pull so tightly around me that it was very difficult to walk.

I saw a herd of horses not far away but at first I had no fear of them; evidently they were curious about me so they came over near me. Blucher would dart after them barking, they would run a little ways and then turn and come back.

I was becoming more and more frightened all the time. I tried again and again to run but each time my skirt would wrap more firmly around my legs. I would stop and unwind it and struggle on.

These wild horses had never seen such a strange looking object as I must have appeared to be and they kept circling and coming after me with Blucher chasing them back until I reached the barbed wire fence and rolled under it.

I was thoroughly frightened for I was not sure whether the horses were merely curious or whether they thought I was some kind of a wild animal that they should dispatch by trampling me to death.

Soon after I got home I heard a friendly "hello"! When I opened the door, I found our rancher friend and his wife standing there. They had come over to spend the evening with me. I think I can truthfully say that no guests were ever more welcome. I insisted that they should stay over night with me, which they did and we talked until long after midnight. It was such a rare treat to have interesting guests in our house.

They told me to take the bandages off my dog. That a dog would take care of his own wounds far better than I could do it for him.

I took their advice and since Blucher was well very soon, I was very happy that I had done so.

The hot weather had dried up the water hole near the house until I felt that we should no longer use the water from it. Accordingly, I carried water for the house use from a water hole that was fed from a spring. This was about a quarter of a mile away and I found it most difficult to carry a pail of water such a distance. Then I thought of taking two one gallon syrup pails and carrying one in each hand to balance the burden. This simplified things but it did not provide a very generous supply of water. It seemed to me that I would just get to the house with fresh water when some one would stop and want a drink. I would tell them about the spring, but they would usually say, "Why lady, I only want a cup full."

The road between Cottonwood and Philip went right by our door and some days it seemed to me that I did little else than carry water for these strange people.

One day a whole wagon load of people drew up before the door and asked for water. A big burly German was driving the team. As I turned to go into the house to get the water he started to get down out of the wagon. I told him quickly that he better stay in the wagon as my dog was very cross to strangers. The man looked down at Blucher and said, "Oh, he will not hurt me." About that time he put his foot on the ground and Blucher grabbed him by the hip. The dog did not break the skin but he gave the man a good pinch so that he scrambled quickly back into the wagon rubbing his bruised hip and saying, "Oh mine Gott! Oh, mine Gott!" Then he looked at Blucher where he sat on my feet, his hair standing up and his teeth showing, and he said, "But, he is a fine dog, lady, I'll give you five hundred dollars for that dog."

I answered, "No, Mister, I will not sell him for any money. He is no common dog. I have raised him as though he were a child. I would just as soon think of selling a human being as to sell him." One of the women in the wagon said, "I would like to have some man offer me five hundred dollars for a dog and then watch how quickly I would take it."

These people had begun to make me cross and I said, "That would be your priviledge, madam, but perhaps we have a different view point."

They had drunk up all the water I had at the house by this time and as they were driving up the hill across Meyers' draw Blucher and I started on another pilgrimage to the spring to carry water for the thirsty people who stopped. Some of whom were so ungrateful that they would never even say, "Thank you."

Sunday when John was at home he made a seat for me out of an old stump under a willow tree. This made a good resting place when I was coming with water from the spring. I liked the place very much for a mother shrike had her nest in the tree and I liked to watch her work. When I would sit down on the stump, she would leave her nest and come out on the limb and scold and scold at me.

I never was able to decide whether she was scolding at me for my apparent intrusion on what she might have considered her domain or whether she was just an ordinary female scold.

One night early in August we had one of the most furious thunder storms that I have ever witnessed. I was awakened from a sound sleep by such a frightful clap of thunder that I felt that the lightning must have struck near by. I looked out of the window and by the lightning flashes I could see the background of the sky was green, with wind clouds rolling our direction. Then the storm broke in all its fury. I have never seen more vivid lightning or heard

Pioneers of 1907 taking time out from hay baling to eat watermelons. (Photo courtesy Mrs. Anna Burjes,
First Half Century, Philip, South Dakota*)*

such awful thunder. The wind blew with so much violence that it seemed that the roof would be lifted off the dug out. The timbers creaked and then settled back. The next gust of wind would pull and tug at the roof until I was panic stricken, and waited almost breathlessly between these awful gusts of wind for I felt that undoubtedly the next one would unroof the house. It did not seem best to have a light so I sat shivering in the darkness. I pulled Blucher's stool up by my chair and it was a comfort to feel his little warm body against me.

The storm had scarcely died down when I heard men's voices calling. I put on my coat over my night gown and drew on my rubber boots and went into the yard. I could see a lantern light on the other side of Meyers' draw and could hear Bill Smith calling, "Hey, are you all right? Did the roof blow off from your house?" I assured him that I was all right but he kept on calling, "What's the matter? Anything wrong?" I was shrieking assurances that I was quite all right when I heard Paul's voice saying, "We are all right, but we are coming over there before the water gets so high in the draw that we can't get across."

Paul and I had both been answering Bill at the same time. Bill had heard me and knowing that I was all right, he did not come across the draw, but Paul had not heard me at all. In just a moment here they were, he and June. They were only about half dressed and poor June as white as a sheet, and was sobbing and crying. Their shack was just setting up on piles of stones until Paul could find time to make the foundation. This terrible storm had rocked it so badly that they felt sure that it would blow over. As soon as the storm abated they had started for our house feeling that the dug out would be safer.

Poor little June, she seemed so tiny that she was like a little child, kept sobbing, "Oh why do we stay in this terrible country. It is nothing but one awful thing after another." I assured her that such is the life of pioneers, but she refused to be comforted, so I made up the extra bed for Paul and took her in my bed. I held her in my arms until she got warm and went off to sleep. The light of dawn came in at the window and showed her rumpled auburn hair on the pillow. Her tiny little face, still almost colorless, touched my heart with pity. I knew then that pioneering was not the life for one as frail as she.

They stayed with me until late afternoon the next day, waiting for the water to run down Meyers' draw, then as they went home I walked as far as the willow tree with them for I wondered how my mother shrike had weathered the storm. She came out on the limb and scolded at me as usual. When I got back to the house I wrote this:

THE SHRIKE'S NEST

The mother shrike had built her nest
In an old twisted willow tree down by the garden
The baby birds were hatched
But not yet old enough to fly

The mother bird, as women folks are prone to do,
Fretted and scolded and fussed
Yet worked incessantly all day
Her hungry brood to feed
At night she held them close beneath her downy wings.

The evening breeze gently rocked the willow tree
That housed the mother shrike
And her fuzzy nestlings
Baby birds like these.

The night wore on, a storm came up
It shook the willow tree

With all the fierce intensity
Of an infuriated demon

But still the patient mother bird
Sat on her nest
And hugged her fuzzy babies tight
Beneath her downy wings

Does God forget his nestlings
In such a plight as this
Do they trust Him in times like these?
Who knows?

The storm ceased with the dawn
The mother shrike took up her endless round of duties
How did she thank her Maker for His care through storms?
Who knows?

Paul said that he must put a substantial foundation under his shack
before they were obliged to live through any more such experiences
with wind storms.

There were plenty of flat stones to use for this purpose and Paul
being an excellent mason, he began hauling stones at once. By the
following Saturday he was ready for the cement. He said if he could
use one of our horses he would take one of his and bring John home
with him on the load of cement.

Of course I was happy to make such an arrangement for June
had promised to spend the day with me while Paul was away.

They came over Saturday morning before I had had my breakfast and Paul was on his way to town soon after that.

Before noon a heavy cloud came up in the west and by one o'clock we were having a regular cloud burst. Since this storm came from the west there was no danger of our roof's blowing off and June was not badly frightened, but as soon as the rain ceased I went out to see if it had done any damage.

Sure enough, water was coming down the draw by the barn in a perfect torrent and was running into the barn very badly. I waded in the water way above my knees and led our other horse out and tied her to the wagon which happened to be standing on high ground.

I changed my clothes and we were taking turns reading aloud to each other when June looked out of the window and saw two men coming toward the house. They had a very large dog with them.

She was panic stricken. She said, "If they are just common tramps they can never come in here. Hurry and lock the door while I get the guns ready."

I went over to close the door but I found that in going in and out I had left so much mud on the threshold that I was obliged to scrape it away before I could get the door closed.

While I was stooping over, I hear the report of a gun and a bullet whizzed past me and lodged in the sod wall above my head, followed by bullet number two before I could catch my breath.

"June! June! Turn that gun the other way!" I shouted for I had realized in an instant that she had Paul's repeating rifle in her hands and since it had started to go off she did not know what to do.

She obeyed me and turned the gun into the spare bed that stood next to the wall. She knew that she should not shoot that to pieces so she turned the gun against the wall. By the time I got to her she had emptied the magazine of the gun. The bed and the muslin that I had put all around the room on the sod walls to make the house look clean, were on fire and poor June was ready for hysterics.

Fortunately there was plenty of water in the house. It took only a few moments to put out the fire in the muslin, but it took a longer time to smother the fire in the bed and to comfort June. She kept saying over and over "If I had killed you, no one would have believed that I did not do it on purpose. Circumstantial evidence would have been against me."

I hugged her up in my arms and told her not to feel badly that it was only an accident and that I was not hurt. When she stopped crying she helped me to carry the smoking bed clothes out into the yard and to get the house in order after our fire.

It was not until then that we realized that we had entirely forgotten the men who had caused all this commotion. They had not come to the house, nor were they any where in sight. We learned afterwards that they were some men who had homesteads several miles above us on Meyers' draw. The storm had delayed their going home until they were afraid they would get lost if they went directly across the prairie and they had come down to Meyers' draw near our house and then followed it on to their homes.

John and Paul did not get home until long after dark for John had been obliged to work late and then they were forced to go several miles out of their way to find a place where the water was shallow enough in Meyers' draw for them to cross. When we told them what had happened they were thoroughly disgusted with us. They did not give us a bit of sympathy but each of them gave us a good scolding just as though we were two small children.

I wrote to Mother as soon as my garden was destroyed and told her of my loss. She knew how much the garden had meant to me and how hard I had worked to make a success of it. As she had a very splendid garden soon after the fourth of July she gathered some new peas, dug some new potatoes, pulled turnips, carrots and beets until she thought she had about all the garden stuff that I could use before it would get stale. Then she and Anne hired the buggy and horses that they had used at Thanksgiving time and brought their treat over to me. They arrived very early Sunday morning. John was even more pleased than I was to see them for his conscience still hurt him about that garden fence.

I told them about Blucher's accident the night he chased the cattle out of the garden and how I had swathed him in bandages until my rancher friend told me to take them off so that the dog could get well. Anne looked at once so disgustedly and said, "I've always been thankful that he is only a dog."

We will be obliged to make some changes in our living plans soon. Blucher and I have held down the homestead for five months alone. Some different arrangements must be made soon. I shall write to you after we decide definitely on a plan.

Lovingly,
Tully

Proving Up

October 5, 1907

My dear Sara:

It seems that the most outstanding things that have happened since I wrote to you last are the separations caused by proving up. No, I do not mean divorces. I mean that many people have proved up on their land and left it. Some have gone into Philip, while others have left this part of the country. Those who have sold the land, have no doubt, gone away to live. Perhaps others hope to work elsewhere and get money enough to stock their places, or it may be they plan to come back and do dry farming.

Since you asked me in your last letter to explain what constitutes proving up, I shall try to be more explicit. The government opened for settlement a part of the Sioux Indian Reservation between Pierre and Rapid City. I do not know just how much land was included in this opening, but there were at least several thousand acres. A person who wished to file on this land was obliged to go before a United States Land Commissioner and make out his filing papers. These papers contained a statement that the person had seen the land and that he agreed to take up residence within six months, and that at the end of eight months he could again appear before a United States commissioner with three bona fide witnesses who were willing to swear that the homesteader had made his homestead his home for at least eight months. After paying fifty cents an acre for the land, the United States government will issue him a patent to the land. There is a second plan for proving up which a few people use.

Under this plan the homesteader maintains his residence on the land for five years. During this time his land is free from taxation because it still belongs to the government. At the end of the five years, the person who wishes to use this plan must appear before the United States Commissioner with his witnesses who are willing to swear that he has made this his home for five years. He may then get a patent for his land.

These conditions seemed so easy, and the prospect of getting one hundred and sixty acres of land for fifty cents an acre, and a residence requirement of eight months, seemed so very alluring, that many people did not stop to actually count the cost of such an undertaking, but rather assumed that they would be taken care of in some way. Accordingly they filed on a piece of land, established residence, made the necessary improvements, and found that they had very little money left to live on for the eight months.

Apparently we were no exception to this rule. Although we had counted the cost very carefully before we came, we found that our estimate fell far short of the actual cost, and it would be necessary for one, or both of us, to work and earn money to finance any further improvements on the land. John was working in the bakery but he could not seem to save any money at all. Each week he would think that he would be able to save some out of his next week's wages; but after several months of this struggling, we realized that we would need to make some other arrangement.

The school board of the Philip district had offered me the school again for next year, and it seemed to us that this might be a way out.

John, however, was very much opposed to proving up on the eight months plan. He seemed to fear that if we once left the place that we would never go back there to make our home. Still he was not happy to be in town at work leaving me alone on the homestead with my dog. Five months of that sort of life was all that I cared for, so we decided to prove up and move into town before school opened in the fall. As Paul and June could not prove up until March, we made arrangements with them to take care of our horses, cows, and two calves.

I think I did not tell you that we called our first calf "Butinsky" because she bunted the bucket so hard when we fed her. Then John bought a calf at six weeks old for three dollars. She was black all over so I called her "Coaly." The calves were old enough by the time that we proved up so that June said she could care for them and would be glad to do it for it would make her responsible for something that was alive. June thought that the calves should be free to get a drink whenever they wanted one, but if she turned them loose, they would go up to the corn field.

I brought her out some halters and ropes so that she could stake the calves out. One night she staked "Coaly" near a water hole that had a very steep bank on one side, but there was a good path leading down to the water on the other side of the hole.

June said, "I thought any animal had sense enough to follow a path down to the water." Perhaps "Coaly" thought that a short cut would do just as well, at any rate, she walked off the steep bank and hung herself.

Paul and June could not be induced to take care of the animals any longer so that it was necessary to make other arrangements until we could get a barn built down town. Accordingly, one neighbor took the horses to work for their keep until he could finish up his fall work, while another neighbor took the cow and calf.

Soon after John had gone to work in the bakery in the spring, I had bought two pigs with some of my school money. I thought that I could feed them on weeds and extra vegetables from my garden together with what milk we did not need for house use. They proved to be a nuisance for I soon learned that a pig does not care to stay in a pen and when he is at liberty, he is a perfect pest.

Paul found them in my garden one day and brought them back and put them in the pen. Bill Smith found them down Meyers' draw about a half mile from the house. He brought them back and put them in the pen. The next Sunday, John found them in the barn eating the grain we had stored there for the horses. I was glad each time that there had been a man about the place so that I had not been obliged to help put the pigs back into the pen.

About this time, a neighbor living several miles away came for Paul to plaster his house. June and I insisted that he should go for then she could come over and stay with me.

I think you know, Sara, that Anne left just as soon as she proved up on her homestead for as she intended to enter the Normal school when the fall term opened, she was obliged to leave here before Mother could prove up.

June and I were not half sorry to have Anne go for then we thought we would have a chance to have Mother with us more. We planned to take turns staying with her on her claim and then to bringing her over to our homes for a part of the time.

As soon as Paul left for his plastering job, June went over to Mother's claim and brought her over to spend the time with us. We stayed at my house for it was larger and I had an extra bed. One evening, June and I went over to a neighbor's who lived about three quarters of a mile to the south of us to see if he would bring us some groceries when he went to town the next day. These people were very cordial and entertained us by playing on an accordion and singing Hungarian folk songs. We did not realize that the time was passing so quickly, as it was after ten before we knew it.

We bid them goodnight and started for home at once, wondering what Mother would think. She always wanted us to be in the house before dark, for fear that we would get lost. We were far from brave as we hurried along toward home. All at once we clutched each other closely for right before us in a clump of weeds in the bed of the draw was a dark object which moved as we came near it.

There was no other way to get to the house but to pass that clump of weeds, so at last we started on. As we did so the animal in the weeds moved and started toward us. Then we saw that it was a pig. While we were still chuckling to ourselves over our nonsense at being frightened at a pig, the second one ran past us. We clutched each other again and then began to laugh, but June said, "Hush, don't let any one know about this, for we do not want them to have a chance to tease us about being afraid of a pig."

We knew so little about pig nature that we vainly imagined that we could shoo them back into the pen as you would chickens. They refused to shoo, and scampered off in opposite directions, running much faster than we could. Finally we were able to get one down near the pen. June said, "You go slowly one way around the pen and I'll go the other. When we get him between us we will both grab him." We slipped stealthily around the pen with the unsuspecting pig between us and soon we were close enough to him so that we both made a grab for him. Our feet slipped out from under us on the slick grass and we sat facing each other roaring with laughter, while the pig ran off a short distance and stopped.

I said, "June, why didn't you hang on to him?"

"Why, I couldn't. My hand slipped off from his back. Why didn't you hold him?"

I said, "I couldn't. There was nothing on his neck to hold on to."

Mother heard us laughing and came to the door. She called to us to know what we were doing. We told her the pigs were out and that we were trying to get them back in the pen. She came out to where we were still seated on the grass laughing. When we told her that one of us had tried to catch the pig by the back and other one by the neck, she was disgusted and said, "I supposed either of you knew enough to catch a pig by the ears or hind legs." She put some feed in the trough, calling to the pigs as she did so. They went into the pen without any further difficulty.

We told Mother that she was a real pioneer, as she thought the difficult situation that we had in mind, simply called for common sense. We frankly admitted that she might be right at that. It takes a member of your own family to put romantic situations into the realm of the common place.

The next morning about five o'clock we were awakened from a sound sleep by some one pounding on the door and shouting,

"Please get up quick and get ready to come over to our house. My wife is sick and I will go back and get the team and take you over before I go for the doctor." Mother recognized the voice at once as of Mr. Zaruski, the neighbor on the south, where June and I had spent the evening before. She said very calmly, "Don't be frightened Mr. Zaruski, I suppose your wife is about to deliver her child." He said, "Yes, and here we are way off here on these God forsaken prairies, miles away from a doctor. If my wife dies, I shall never forgive myself for bringing her here."

Mother told him to go on back home and stay with his wife until she chould get there. She told him that it would only take her a few minutes to dress and that she would be there almost as soon as he would.

June and I were sitting up in bed with our arms around each other saying, "Oh isn't this terrible for her to be so sick away out here." Mother soon put a stop to our wailing by telling us to hurry and get up and dress and get a good fire going so that we would have plenty of hot water. She said for one of us to stay at home and keep up the fire, but for the other one to come on over to Zaruski's as she might need help. June told me to go over to help Mother as she would much prefer the job of fire builder.

I followed Mother in what seemed to me to be an incredibly short time, but as I cautiously opened the door, I heard a baby's cry so I closed the door and waited out side. After a while Mother came out and told me to go on back home, for everything was over soon after she arrived. The Zaruskis had a fine baby girl and that they were not going to have a doctor as everything was all right with both mother and child.

Mother came home shortly afternoon and said that she had promised to go over each morning and take care of Mrs. Zaruski and her baby which they had named Mersaydes. I could not help from saying, "Of all names in a place like this. If I had been naming her, I should have called her either Faith, Hope or Charity."

As soon as Mrs. Zaruski was able to be about the house again, Mother thought that she had better go back to her homestead. When Paul had finished his plastering job and was at home again, I told June I would go over and stay with Mother for a few days.

We got to town shortly after noon and went directly to the bakery to see John. One glance at his face told me that something was wrong. He said, "I am glad you are here for I was just making arrangement for some one to come out for you. We have received word that Anne's shack is burning." This was quite a blow to Mother for she had provisions enough stored there to last until she could prove up, as well as enough wood and coal to last for the same length of time. Besides all this, much of her bedding, as well as her best clothes were in Anne's shack.

Mother stood and looked at John for several minutes. When she spoke her voice was very calm. She said, "I am very sorry for the loss of all the things which I can so ill afford to lose at this time, but I feel much worse to think that there is a man living who would be so mean as to do a shameful thing like this to an old woman like me. So far as I know, I have no enemies, for to my knowledge, I have never wronged any one in my life."

It seemed incredible that any one could have really set this shack on fire. Anne was full of spirit, but surely she had made no enemies. At any rate, she had proved up on her land and gone. Why anyone

Lucy Bowen, mother of Tully.
(family photo)

would want to make trouble for a dear old lady like my mother was something no one could understand. Mother and I went over to Anne's place only to find that the fire had undoubtedly been set. The plowed ground for Mother's garden surrounded the house and there was no evidence of fire either in the garden or beyond it although the wood pile and coal pile were still burning when we got there.

Feeling ran high among the neighbors. They had felt so secure in their little homestead shacks; and now that this thing had happened, no one would feel safe to leave home for fear of being burned out. The men rode into the place by two's and three's for several days. They would talk earnestly with Mother about the fire and try to get her to express some opinion as to whom she thought set the fire. One man went so far as to say that if she knew who did it, he would be one to head up a "neck-tie party" for him.

Poor Mother was terrified at such a thought. She said that she did not know now who had set the fire and she hoped that she never would, for she would not want to know a person who harbored such evil thoughts.

Beth, June and I shared our meager supplies with her so that we were able to fix her shack up very comfortably for her use until she could prove up. Then we made arrangements for one of our young women friends to stay with her so that she would never be left alone. When it was time for her to prove up, I went over and helped her pack up her things ready for shipment. We finished late in the afternoon so we thought we would go on over to Brother Sam's and stay all night.

The next morning he brought us over and was planning to take mother's things to the railroad station. When we neared mother's shack, we thought it did not look just right. Surely enough, some one had been there and stolen her door and window.

None of her personal belongings seemed to have been disturbed. We took this as a threat to leave and not come back. We felt a sense of relief when she had finally made proof on her land and no violence had been done to her person. She thought perhaps it would be better for her to go back to our old home for the winter. When we bade her good bye at the station she said, "There have been many changes since I came here over a year ago. Some things have been rather hard, but on the whole, I think it has been a delightful experience for a woman to have had when she has reached my years."

Such a wonderful mother! Seventy years of age, a clear thinker, spry, young at heart, and the spirit of the pioneers strong within her.

Brother Sam proved up next. His daughter Lucy was old enough to go to school. There was no school near enough for her to attend so they left for their home in Kansas soon after they had made final proof.

The merchants in Philip were using public auction as an advertising scheme. They hired an auctioneer and held an auction every Saturday. This gave people who wished to leave the country a chance to get a little money out of their household goods and those who were just coming into the country a chance to buy things very cheaply.

Bill Smith took advantage of one of these auctions. He sold his belongings in this way soon after he made final proof on his land. He left at once as he said he wanted to get back to Nebraska in time to pick corn in order to live during winter.

June and Paul have decided to stay on here. They hope to make this their permanent home. Paul has dug a well and found good water. He walled the well up with rock so it will not cave in. He also plastered their shack so that they will be quite comfortable this winter. We have proved up and will move into Philip just as soon as John can find a house for us to live in.

I shall write you in detail about this new town of Philip in my next letter.

Lovingly,
Tully

The New Town

October 20, 1907

My dear Sara:

I do not wonder that in your last letter you asked me to tell you something about our new town. To do this I shall have to start back about the time we came on to our homestead.

The Pierre and Rapid City railway company owned all the town sites along the rail road and there seemed to be a great deal of uncertainty just where the town of Philip would be located. Everyone seemed to think that Philip would be the best town between Pierre and Rapid City. That was a very logical conclusion for it would be about half way between these two cities. The fact that it was to be located at the forks of North and South Bad River would assure plenty of water. That last fact is an item of great importance in this semi-arid country. The government reports made before opening this tract for settlement showed an average rain fall of between twelve and eighteen inches annually.

The rail way company held out the inducement to settlers that they would sink artesian wells at the principal town sites and this way provide an ample supply of water. They kept this part of their agreement at Capa and Nowlin, two towns between Philip and Fort Pierre, but when they came to Philip, they secured such an

115 ~

abundant flow of good water at a reasonable depth that they abandoned the artesian well project. The town so far has an abundant supply of good water from shallow wells. The better class of citizen is already talking of a water works system to reduce the fire hazard. Fires are surely the greatest enemy of frontier towns.

The rail way company finally announced the location of the Philip town site but refused to have a lot sale before the railway was completed into Philip. Accordingly the more ambitious business people who were planning on locating in the new town put up temporary shacks along the banks of Bad River. These they intended to move to their lots as soon as they were able to buy them.

The town site was to be some where on a narrow flat that lay between the Bad River on the south and a line of bluffs on the north while the North Fork of Bad River might be the western boundary and as the line of bluffs curved to the east it was quite likely that this would form the eastern boundary.

This whole stretch was about two and a half miles long therefore Philip will be some sizable village when it fills all this space. The bluffs to the north and east are easy of access. No doubt the residential section will be up there in the near future.

The lot sale took place on May 9th, the day that the railroad was completed into Philip and the first train came over the rails. When it came to the buying of the lots, the excitement ran high to see which business men would be able to get the corner lots for these were the most desirable.

It seemed to be generally agreed that the new town should have two main streets, the one to be called Railroad street was to parallel

Immediately after the town lot sale the race began to see who
would be the first to get his business located on the townsite.
The buildings housing the **Bad River News** *and the* **Warner Land Co.**
were loaded and waiting for the end of the sale.
The **Bad River News** *won, locating on Lot 14, Block 6 on Oak Street.*
*(***First Half Century, Philip, South Dakota***)*

the railroad track, while the one called Main street was to cut it at
right angles about opposite the depot site.

This lot sale was like a game of checkers to me. Since I was not
buying a lot, I did not have access to the inner workings of the plan,
but I was intensely interested for some of these people who were
buying, I had learned to count as real friends. Knowing full well that
the location of a business house may mean the success or failure of
that business my friends' interests became my interests for the day.

In jostling about in the crowd, I would hear first one rumor and
then another. Some one would say, "The hotel is to be on the corner

diagonally across the street from the depot." Then I would mentally put the hotel there. "The post office is to be across the street from the depot facing the hotel." Then I would put the post office there. Perhaps the next rumor would have these places taken by a store and a bank. You can see how much fun it was to play this mental checker game all after noon with imaginary houses for the men. I could almost hear my opponent say, "Your move."

Then something really happened. The lot buyers adjusted their differences and the rush began to see which building would be the first to be moved onto the new town site.

Many of these temporary business houses, or more properly speaking, shacks, were blocked up. One of these, Mr. Jenkins store out on the banks of North Fork, where we had traded ever since coming into this country. This store had been the trading post of this ranch country for many years. I think many people hoped that this store would be the first to reach the town site, for it really seemed right that it should have this place in the history of the town. The other building was the temporary quarters of the *Bad River News* office. This building was only a shack located on the banks of the Bad River about as far to the east of town as Mr. Jenkin's store was west of town.

The man who told me that the bob cat at the old Philip post office was stuffed was the editor of the *Bad River News*. He was a great favorite among his friends and they were eager to see his building the first to be moved to the new town site.

As the strange race between these two houses got under way, the crowd became divided in its sympathies. Many of us who were friends of the Jenkins family walked out to where this building was

The **Bad River News** *office was the first building
to move onto the new town site.*
(First Half Century, Philip, South Dakota)

and urged the men and horses to hurry so that his pioneer store would reach the town site first.

A similar group who were interested in seeing the *Bad River News* office reach the town site went to where that building was being moved and urged those men to put forth every effort to get that building on the town site first.

It was great fun to participate in this excitement. When one building would forge ahead a short distance, the crowd that surrounded it would shout, while the men would throw up their hats into the air to show their appreciation of the efforts of the men and horses that were doing the work. Many a good natured bet was made by these enthusiastic citizens.

Some of the men who had put up money on the Jenkins' store brought up fresh horses to the men who were doing the moving job. As soon as these horses were hitched to the building, they walked right away with it so that it was far ahead in the race when without any warning several joists under the floor gave way. This let the building down so that it was necessary to do a considerable amount of repair work on it before it could be moved further.

Our hopes crashed as the floor had done. If Mr. Jenkins had realized the terrible strain that this moving would subject his building to, perhaps he would have removed his stock of goods and then, no doubt, his store would have been the first to reach the town site.

When the floor broke through on Mr. Jenkin's store, the race so far as these two business houses was concerned was over, but the *Bad River News* editor had said that if he had no bad luck, his office would be on the town site by sun down. So the race continued with the news office and the sun as competitors. I am very happy to say that the *Bad River News* won for just as the sun was going down, the steaming horses pulled the news office on to the new location and the editor hastily hoisted the stars and stripes above the building. Eureka! he had won. The *Bad River News* office was the first building to move on to the new town site. The town of Philip had been definitely located. It was to be only a matter of a few days until all the temporary buildings would be moved over to their new locations and the work started on making permanent buildings, or fixing up the temporary buildings so that they would more nearly meet the needs of the new town.

I suppose this is a typical frontier town for these temporary buildings are all unpainted. Some of them have the new lumber exposed while others have the roof and sides covered either with tar paper or blue building paper.

There is an immense amount of business transacted here every day for these business men are keen and wide awake to the opportunities that the opening of this reservation has brought to them by bringing in all these people either as homesteaders or curious land seekers.

Since the railroad has been completed into Philip there is an ever increasing number of people coming here all the time. Some are coming on horse back, some in wagons, but by far the greater number are coming on the train.

These people have waited to be certain that the railroad was actually built into this western country. They also wanted to make sure that this part of the Souix reservation was tillable land suitable for farming. Of course, this influx of people brought a very great many adventurers. Some of these people hoped to make personal gains out of the losses of their more unfortunate fellows. It is not an unusual thing for people to come here with high hopes and little capital. When their capital is gone, they have no means of replenishing their supply and consequently are forced to sell out for what ever they can get for their holdings.

The unscrupulous land seekers are ever alert to buy these filings that have some improvements for much less than the improvements cost. He can resell to the land hungry and make a very good profit.

Then again there are many people who had no intention of making proof on the land when they filed on it. They would file and then before the six months expired, when it would be necessary for them to establish residence, they would sell their relinquishment. If their filing happened to be a desirable one, they would often make several hundred dollars over and above their filing fees. Beside these, there are the people who had over estimated their moral courage. It really takes moral courage to leave a comfortable home and come out on to the frontier where there are no comforts of any kind and put up with the hardships which must come when you are living in houses devoid of all conveniences.

There is something about the life in the vast expanse of the prairies which seems to appeal to the men. The spirit of adventure is so firmly planted in them that they like a contest of any kind. The contest for life in this new, untried country satisfies this love of adventure to some extent. They get a thrill out of the living.

With the women it is quite a different proposition. Some of them make such brave attempts to establish livable homes here, but the truth finally bears in upon them that these are only make shifts, for the first generation of pioneers has the hardships while the second generation reaps the benefits. When you meet a woman who has the heart hunger in her eyes, you know that the homesickness has begun and sooner or later that family would be leaving this country. Often the wife goes "back home" to visit her family. Sometimes she comes back satisfied to stay on a while longer, but when she has once had a case of real homesickness, the new country has lost its appeal and she is no longer willing to live in this primitive fashion, and the family returns to the old home, or else they go where they can have the comforts this civilization affords.

You can see from all this that there is a constant stream of people coming and going in and out of Philip all the time. It is the job of this little frontier town to minister to the needs of all these people.

Shortly after the town lot sale the street going west from
Center Avenue looked like this. The Bank of Philip was housed
in the wooden structure on the corner. Next to it is the Philip
Hardware and then Hoffman's restaurant, the **Bad River News,**
F. A. Arnolds, Gus's Barn and E. L. Hill horse shoeing.
(Photo courtesy Mrs. Fred Haberly,
First Half Century, Philip, South Dakota)

This may not seem much to you, but think of these crowds of people coming into this little shack town, expecting to be housed and fed while here; then transported to their filings no matter how far away they may be. Materials must be provided for improving their land and also food and clothing available for them to live in comfort. The people of Philip took this very large order which this shifting population had placed upon them and they certainly are filling the order with credit to themselves and all concerned. They are such an admirable group of people. They have settled all their differences in an amicable fashion as they did the choice of lots at the lot sale. They said, "We will pull together to make Philip the best town between Pierre and Rapid City. If we have any differences of opinion we will settle them among ourselves, but to the outside world we are as one person."

They have lived up to that code which, I think, tells you something of the type of person who is helping to make Philip a real town. They are as fine a group of people as you will meet anywhere. They are keen, wide awake, hard working, and public spirited. That kind of folks should make a good town anywhere.

As the town stands now the Bank of Philip is on the corner of Railroad and Main streets, diagonally across from the depot with a hardware store next door, a cafe comes next, and then the *Bad River News* office, then a livery and feed barn.

Going the opposite direction down Railroad street, you will find a large saloon on the corner opposite the Bank of Philip with three other smaller saloons following along one after the other down the street, making saloon row. All of these saloons have the part of their lots at the rear that is not used by the building, enclosed in a high board fence reaching back to the alley. Perhaps it is just as well that they have taken this precaution. These high board fences are certainly unsightly, but they may hide things that are far more unsightly. You may draw your own conclusions about that.

On Main street across the alley from this corner saloon is the Northwestern hotel. Mr. Jenkin's store stands next with a temporary post office next to that. Two general stores complete this side of the block.

From the November 6, 1908 issue of the **Philip Weekly Review**
came the following article about the Northwestern Hotel:
"The Northwestern Hotel, Lindsay and Orr, proprietors, has recently
completed the large two-story cement structure shown above.
The hotel as it is now, entailed a cost of $20,000. There are 40 rooms.
The dining room service is highly commended. The place is popular
with commercial men and the traveling public."
(First Half Century, Philip, South Dakota)

Starting a new block, is a land office and a tiny postal card shop.
Just across Main street from these is a long rooming house, with the
United States Land Commissioner's office standing next to it on the
corner. Across the street on the corner is the First State Bank, going
on down Main street toward the depot you will come to a general

store, a drug store, candy store, land office and rooming house. This brings us back to the Bank of Philip corner.

Right back of the United States Commissioner's office is a large hall where we hold most of the community meetings. It has a good hard maple floor so that it is used for dancing. You could not think of a frontier town without its dance hall.

Standing just across the alley from this dance hall is a two story building. The down stairs is used for a general store while in the upstairs is the living quarters of the proprietor's family.

There are five two story buildings, the Northwestern hotel, one lodging house, the drug store, and two general stores. The rest of the buildings are one story frame structures. A few of them are sided up and painted, but most of them are covered with sheet iron or building paper.

The newness of it all holds a great fascination for me. I like the smell of the new lumber, the new paint, and believe it or not, I like the smell of the tar paper they sometimes use to cover the side and roofs of these new buildings.

I don't want you to think that I am complaining for I do not mean it that way, but I was extremely lonely on the homestead with just my dog as a house mate. He is a good trusty companion but he can not talk and the stillness of it all got on my nerves at times.

It was a real treat to come down to Philip. Since John worked at the hotel, I always made headquarters there. It was my delight to take care of the hotel office for then I could see the people at close range. Often they would stop at the desk and talk with me. Each person was so intent on the thing that he was about to undertake. He felt so confident that his particular undertaking was going to be the means of his making some good money. Far be it from me to discourage them.

I liked to step out into the hotel kitchen at meal time. It seemed to me that the dish washer tried to see how much noise he could make in rattling the silver and slamming the dishes about. The waitresses used to shout out their orders so rapidly, yet loudly to be heard above the rattle of the dish washing, while all the available help dashed here and there trying to fill the orders quickly, or to keep a plentiful supply of clean dishes ready for the serving.

In the dining room, every one seemed eager to be served at once so that he could eat in a hurry and take up the endless round of rushing here and there getting ready to leave town as quickly as possible.

No one regretted that people were in a hurry to get away for that left room for the others who kept crowding in to take any vacant places, each one demanding food, shelter, money, clothes, supplies and service.

How patiently and willingly these people gave this service amidst all this crowding, jostling, hurrying, hurrying. Every one always in a hurry.

One day I had ridden into town with June and Paul. June and I had cashiered in the hotel offices during the noon rush and had enjoyed it immensely. In fact, we had been busy until late afternoon, when we took our bundles of groceries and sat down on a bench outside the hotel office door to wait for Paul to drive up for us.

June sat facing the corner saloon. All at once, she said, "Something is wrong, something must have happened in that saloon." I looked up and saw a large crowd of men coming out on to the street. A woman screamed and dashed across the street and into the midst of the crowd. As they moved up the street toward us, we realized that they were coming to the hotel. June and I gathered up our bundles quickly and went up in front of Mr. Jenkin's store so that we would be out of the way. As the crowd approached us, we saw that the woman who had run across the street was supporting a gray haired man, while other men were trying to help the old man along. When they turned to go into the hotel, we could see the blood on the back of the old man's head. We thought he had been shot and we were trying to elbow ourselves into the crowd hoping to find out the particulars of the case, when Paul drove up and said, "Come on, let us get out of here. This is no place for you folks."

I will admit that we left rather reluctantly. Although I whispered to June as we were leaving, "Never mind, I'll find out all about it from John when he comes home Saturday night."

Paul drove along for a mile or more without saying a word. We had not questioned him about the affair, for we did not think he knew any more than we did; but finally, he could not longer resist the temptation to tell us what he knew about the exciting incident.

It seems that the old gray haired man had a big sheep ranch up north of Philip. He and several of his ranch hands brought his wool in town that day. After he had paid the men their wages, he had taken them all over to the saloon and treated them. He had discharged one of his sheep herders and they had brought him along to town so that he could leave on the train. The rancher and the sheep herder had some differences of opinion about the herders wages that he had coming to him. They had talked for some time about the affair,

~ 128

apparently going over the account together. The herder was still dissatisfied and insisted upon a settlement upon his terms. At this point, the rancher threw the money down on the table, the amount which he felt rightfully belonged to the man and said, "Take it or leave it just as you please, it don't make a d——— bit of difference to me what you do. I am through with you."

The rancher joined the rest of his men at the bar but the herder, after putting his money in his pocket, went down to the other end of the bar by himself. The bar tender was just setting a couple of glasses down before some late comers when he looked up quickly and said, "Look out there Jack!!" He was too late with his warning, for the herder had come up unnoticed by the side of the two late comers and quick as a flash attempted to stab the rancher in the back, but one of the men standing near struck his arm so that the knife only made an ugly scalp wound in the back of the man's head.

Police! Yes, we had one policeman for all the country lying west of the river. Perhaps it would be better to say that we had one mounted policeman. I do not know what his official title was, but he brought credit to any title for he kept order in this very large territory, not so much by force, as by the fact that men in general respected him so very much. They used to say that they thought he could smell trouble; for it did not matter when a fracas started, he was always there to see the finish. If it was necessary to make an arrest he never failed to get his man.

I am sure I do not know how accurate this cowboy information is, but at any rate, Mr. Policeman rode into Philip while the saloon knifing was on. He arrested the herder before he could get out of the saloon.

Since I know your love for stories, Sara, I am sure you will never be satisfied until you know what sentence these westerners gave to the sheep herder. I trust you do not have a blood thirsty appetite in this instance, for they did not cut his heart out nor string him up to the nearest telegraph pole. On the contrary, the rancher showed the peace officer his accounts and convinced him that he had given the unfortunate man all the money that was coming to him. Then he said, "That boy does not need punishment. He needs to go home and see his folks. He is a fine fellow and a good worker. He has just stayed alone too much with the sheep until he is a little queer. What he needs is to get back into civilization and mix with folks; then he will be all right."

I suppose he had some sort of a trial. I do not know about that, but I know he was not punished.

I was glad to get back to the homestead after all this. June and I said that we would be contented at home for some time for we would have plenty to talk about. The range cattle bothered the homesteader's crops badly. The ranchers had fenced large tracts of land and had put their cattle into these pastures, but the cattle were used to roaming at will and it was hard to keep the fences in good enough condition to hold them in. If one old cow would find a hole in the fence where she could crawl through, she would have the whole herd with her in a short time.

Paul had five acres of good wheat which he thought that he had better fence after my experience with having my garden destroyed. He bought some red cedar posts a few miles beyond Philip and he told June and me that he would take us with him when he went for them. I suggested that if they would leave me in Philip on the way over and stop for me on the way back, I could spend the day at the hotel with John. It was quite a surprise to John and my friends at the hotel when I appeared early one morning and said that I was going to stay all day. They found out by questioning me that Paul was coming back again the next day so they insisted that I should stay over night with them and go back with Paul and June on the following day.

The weather here answers this description:

> "There was a little girl;
> Who had a little curl;
> Right in the middle of her forehead.
> When it is good;
> It is very, very good:
> When it is bad; it is horrid."

I do not agree with the person who said; "South Dakota has only two seasons, winter and August" for the mild weather in spring and fall is almost ideal. During these short sunshiny days the air is crisp and invigorating. Besides the electrical storms of summer and the blizzards of winter, we often have "straight winds." These sometimes blow so strongly that they overturn small buildings and very often take the tops off the haystacks.

On the day that Paul and June left me at the hotel, the wind had been blowing some all day but by late afternoon a "straight wind" was blowing furiously.

It was almost dark when they stopped for me to go home. I told them that I had decided to stay over night in town and go home with them the following day. I urged June to stay with me, but she would not consider it, for she would not allow Paul to make the drive home after dark against that awful wind. I had waited to eat supper with them but as they were too anxious to get home to stop to eat, they hurried away in just a few minutes after they arrived. John and I were eating our supper and I was still fussing about June's having to make that long trip home on such a windy night without having any food, when the fire bell rang. John jumped up from the table and was gone before I could even move or speak. I went out into the hotel office and from the front window I could see the flames shooting up above the two story store building that stood on Pierre street, almost diagonally across the block from the hotel. The wind blowing strongly from that direction was sending showers of fire brands over most of the roofs in the business section of town.

Men, women and children all seemed to be running in the direction of the fire. The terror on the faces of some of them transformed them until you could scarcely recognize them. No wonder they were frightened for all their earthly possessions were in the path of that fire which it seemed humanly impossible to halt.

I seemed like a wooden woman as I stood there watching it all, as if apart from it. The man who washed dishes in the hotel kitchen brought me to my senses about this time. As he rushed past me, he thrust an old flannel shirt into my hands and said, "Don't stand there! Get out into the back yard and watch for fire brands. If any fall near you put them out with this!" I went into the back yard as I was told. There I found a five gallon milk can of water. There were several other milk cans of water placed up and down the alley and other women stationed near them with huge wet rags to beat out the fire brands that fell near them. I walked up and down along the high board fences back of the saloons and around through the hotel yard, waving my rag with the rest. Several brands fell near me, but they were not hard to put out.

As a man came running past me shouted, "Have you plenty of water yet?" I said, "yes, where is the fire? Is it almost under control? Will the town burn?" He called back, "Barn burning! chemicals gone! We will save the town if we can get enough water!"

I was standing in the alley near the fence when he said that. Just then I heard a great noise like a team running away. When they got opposite me, I saw a wagon with some barrels of water in it, one man driving and two men in the back of the wagon with the barrels. The horses were on the dead run, and as the driver lashed them on, the two men in the back of the wagon were evidently trying to keep the barrels from over turning even though water was splashing all over them. All the men were bare headed, their faces were blackened with smoke and their hair was being blown straight back by the awful wind.

This load of water had scarcely passed when I heard another coming, and so on. Then I realized that these men were bringing water from the railroad well or from Bad River—maybe both. They had pressed into service every farmer's wagon, dray wagon, or any other wagon that would hold water barrels. Soon these loads of water barrels passed less frequently and finally they stopped altogether. I knew then that the fire was over. I waited for some time in the darkness for some one to come and tell me that there was no more danger and that I was dismissed from duty; but, as no one came, I went into the hotel office to find out for myself. Really, I think no one had remembered that I was there. The fire was over. The town was saved. What interest could there have been in me?

Just how it all came about, no one knows quite as well as those brave men who fight fire on a volunteer fire department in a small town that can afford only very meagre equipment for fire fighting. John came home much, much later. He, too, seemed to have forgotten that I was in town. His face was so black with smoke that he looked like a negro and his clothes filled the room with the odor of smoke.

He told me that night that it would be necessary for us to live down in the business district during the next year; and since he could not find a house for us, he had rented the rooms over the drug store. He had not been able to save any money at all from his wages and as I had contracted to teach the school for the next year, there seemed to be no other way out. We must live in town and we must live in the business district. I lay awake far into the night thinking about it and trying to formulate some working plans for the future. It rather seemed to me that pioneering, for us, was resolving itself into a stone wall that we could not get over and I was not at all sure that we were going to be able to find a way around. When the school board in Wakefield had again offered me my position as assistant principal in the high school, I said to John, "Perhaps it would be better for us to sell our land and go back home. You could use the money from the land and buy a small business and I will teach until you can get established." But he would not even consider such a move.

At any rate, by the time Paul and June came for me the next evening, I was quite reconciled to John's plan of living in Philip. I scarcely ventured off the homestead for several weeks following my visit to Philip when they had the first fire. Living over a drug store might be necessary, but it certainly was not my idea of our own home that we had planned for all this time. John seemed quite reconciled to it for he liked the bustle of the new town.

He came home one Saturday night and told me that the proprietors of the hotel were obliged to go out of town on business and would be gone for several days. They had asked him if he thought that I would be willing to come into town and stay at the hotel to look after the business for them while they were away. As he was sure I would be willing to do this, he had told them that he would bring me back with him on Sunday afternoon, so that they might leave on the Sunday night train.

I suppose the look on my face betrayed my dread of the responsibility that this undertaking would place upon me, for John added hastily, "They said that you need not hesitate to come because of the danger of fire, for there might be fires in town at any time whether they were at home or not." Thinking, perhaps, that it would be necessary to hold out further inducement to me John said, "There will be church services in town on Sunday afternoon. The Presbyterian missionary for this section of South Dakota will preach. Every one says that he preaches a fine sermon. He must be a fine man for the cowboys come from miles around to hear him. He seems to understand these people out here and they all like him. I am sure that you will enjoy the church services." I did not need any further urging after that for I had not been to church for over a year.

We arrived at the hotel in time for dinner Sunday noon and found several other people there who had driven in from some distance to attend church. John introduced me to the missionary. He is a very large man. Perhaps I should say that he is a very strong man. His build, his carriage, his voice all give you the impression of strength. His large blue eyes, set rather deeply in their sockets, light up with intelligent understanding and a broad genial smile spreads over his face as he greets you. He wears his hair roached back from his high forehead.

No, Sara dear, he does not look like a freak musician or an artist. He simply looks like a good wholesome intelligent American business man.

After dinner, he came into the hotel parlor and visited with John and me until church time. He started his conversation by talking about himself. He said that his parents were Swedish people, but that his mother had died when he was quite a young lad. His father, being a blacksmith, thought that his four boys should be blacksmiths also, and therefore he taught them the blacksmith's trade and did a very thorough job of it in good "old country" fashion. The three brothers found this trade quite satisfactory to them, but our missionary, Mr. David, wanted an education. He said that he had always enjoyed people and even while he was working at his forge in the blacksmith shop, so many people would talk to him about the problems that confronted them in their lives, that he decided to take a theological course and then go into the new western country as a travelling missionary. In this way, he could minister to the people in these outlying districts who would otherwise be deprived of such service. That was why he was in this "west river country" and was going to preach to us.

He was extremely well read. He discussed new books, magazine articles and current events in such an interesting way that we were surprised when he looked at his watch and said, "It is two o'clock—time for church. I shall have to go out and round up the boys for the services."

As he took his hat and left, I said to John, "What does he mean by 'rounding up the boys?'" John laughingly answered, "Oh, he will go down to the saloon and open the door and say, 'Well boys, you have had a good time together, let's all go over to the hall and have church'. The boys will come with him or I will miss my guess."

John guessed correctly. We walked across the street to the building where church was to be held and were talking with some friends in the door way, when John said, "Here they come now." I looked up and sure enough Mr. David was crossing the street toward us followed by ever so many men. They were coming from railroad street and I learned afterwards that Mr. David did go to the saloons and invite them to come to church. They were waiting for him to come to tell them when it was church time. They intended to come to church. That was why so many of them had come into town.

They all respected him and enjoyed hearing him preach. I readily agreed with them for he certainly preached a fine sermon taken from First Corinthians, thirteenth chapter and fourth verse—"Charity suffereth long and is kind."

I have heard many sermons taken from that text but I never have heard one that I enjoyed as I did his. I am sure it was not altogether because I was hungry to hear a sermon. He really had a wonderful message for us all. When services were over, he announced that any who cared to stay for an hour or so of singing would be very welcome. Only a few people left and those of us who stayed had a very good time singing. The room we were using was a vacant store building. Of course, it was not plastered for none of these buildings were plastered yet.

The Dunkirks who lived over their real estate office next door loaned their piano for the services. Mr. David had brought some song books with him. He used a box for a pulpit and the congregation sat on planks placed on nail kegs. We may have been uncomfortable; but we certainly were not conscious of it, for we stayed and sang until we could not see any longer, as there was no way of lighting this building. We talked together in groups for a little while, and since we were all strangers to each other, we took this occasion to get acquainted.

I met the young woman here who is to teach with me in the Philip school. She is charming and I feel sure that we will have a pleasant year together.

The proprietors of the hotel left on the midnight train so that it was necessary for me to be up and about very early Monday morning. I found a great deal to do in planning the meals, buying the provisions, helping the girls who were putting the bed rooms and the rest of the house in order, besides acting as cashier. I felt that I had done a good day's work and had just sat down to rest a few minutes before dinner time when the afternoon train came in. Since a train in these parts was still a novelty, I went to the door and looked out. There was a big crowd of people coming up the street and wondered what could have happened. I did not have long to wonder for they came straight to the hotel and asked for rooms. Then, and not until then, did I realize what a responsibility I had assumed. John knew that all this would happen, for it was an every day occurrance at the hotel, but he thought that I would not have come in to stay for this week if I had really known about the crowd of people that I would have to get lodging for every night.

I was just saying to one man who was registering, "Wait a minute please, for I am not at all sure that we can take care of you, as our rooms are all filled," when John spoke to me and said, "Yes, let them all register. We will take care of them by sending them out into the homes to stay all night." I had not even heard John when he came up beside me, but you just rest assured that I was mighty glad for the assurance that his presence gave me.

People who had never seen each other until that day were forced to share the same room and those who were able to stay at the hotel seemed to feel that they were especially favored.

The job of showing these people where they were going to sleep lasted up until after midnight, for they could not be bothered about where they were going to sleep until they were ready to go to bed. John asked George, the handy man about the house, to stay in the office so that I could go with him when he took the last men to be shown their rooms about two or three blocks away.

It was a bright moonlight night and John and I were strolling along back toward the hotel congratulating ourselves that we were not responsible for finding beds for such a crowd of people every night in the year. As we neared the hotel we heard such loud talking that we knew that something must be wrong, and so we quickened our steps. When we opened the office door we saw a huge fat man lying on and over the edges of an army cot that was placed against the side of the stairway in the office. He was telling George that he or no other blank, blankety blank man could move him from that cot, and that he was the owner of the town site, the railway and goodness only knows what else.

Of course, the truth of the matter was that this huge man was lordly drunk. That much we knew, but we did not know how to get him out of the hotel. George talked, John talked and I talked but he would not move from the cot. As he was so large that the men could not throw him out bodily, there seemed to be only one thing left to do and that was to get the marshal to come and put him out. We did this and I am happy to say that he had enough manhood to come to me the next day and apologize for all the trouble that he had caused the night before.

Tuesday, Wednesday and Thursday were repetitions of Monday, much work, many people, crowded conditions and difficulty in finding places for every one.

Friday morning about two o'clock we were awakened by the most unearthly noises you ever heard, mingled with a man's cries for help. The noise came from a few doors down the hall and in an instant, every man in the hotel was in the hallway. The room door was locked, but John and George broke the door in very quickly. Then found one man in the bed having a violent night mare. In his fright, he had clutched the other man in such a way that he could not move. The man with the night mare was making the frightful noises, while the other man was calling for help, as he was pinioned in such a way that he could not move.

They were perfect strangers to each other as they had never met until that day. They said that they did not care to take a chance on repeating the experience that they had just been through and so they both dressed and went down in the office and sat up until morning.

The rest of us went back to bed but it was a long time before we went to sleep.

The proprietors came home on the afternoon train. Paul and June had come for me and I assure you I was glad to go back to the homestead.

John said that I left about a half hour too soon for they had some more excitement. A man had come into town to haul out some provisions; but after stopping into one of the saloons, he apparently forgot his errand. At any rate, his team had been tied to the hitching rail in front of the saloon all day. When it began to grow dusk, the horses became restless and broke the halter rope with which they were tied and started out. They soon became frightened and bewildered and ran up one street and down the other. No one seemed to be able to stop them until one of the saloon keepers who used to be a cowboy jumped on his horse and rode after the run-a-ways. It was not long before he was able to rope them and quiet them.

I think I shall enjoy living in Philip for I like the people there so very much. Most of the women help their husbands in their stores or other places of business. We will all be starting together and I am very sure that it will be most interesting to "Watch Philip grow."

School will be starting soon. I shall write you in detail about that in my next letter.

Lovingly,
Tully

The Village School

June 25, 1908

My dear Sara:

I told you in my last letter that I would write to you in detail about the school in Philip. I did not realize then that my school life would be so linked up with community life that it would keep me constantly at work during all my waking hours; but such has been the case, and the year has gone by on wings.

The School board told me that school would open on the first Monday in September and so I moved into town and was ready for work on that day, but the school house was far from finished. It seemed to me that the contractor intended to finish every other building in Philip before he started to work on the school house again. As there was no other building available, we were obliged to await his pleasure. At last in sheer desperation, the clerk of the school board said we will open school next Monday morning whether the school house is finished or not.

On the next Monday morning we started school in a school house that had floors and plastered walls but no doors, windows, or casings. Some public spirited person had thought it would be a good idea to have an archway cut between the two rooms so that the school house could be used for public gatherings. The archway had

The Presbyterian church of Philip looked quite alone in the above
shot. This picture was taken on a stormy day in February, 1908.
A. G. Wheeler is in the buggy and others in the picture are
Rev. Bell, Mr. and Mrs. Culp, Mrs. Gearherdt,
Mrs. Wheeler, and Mr. and Mrs. Russell. (Photo courtesy
H. G. Wheeler, **First Half Century, Philip, South Dakota**)

been cut in the wall, but no provision had been made for closing it. No school furniture had arrived yet for the opening of school on Monday. We had the text books that we had used in our country school, but there were not nearly enough of them to go around.

The things that I have mentioned might have been real obstacles if this had been an older community, where teachers and children alike have been accustomed to have things perfectly ordered in good school room fashion.

In this new country every one was used to doing the best that he could with what ever materials he had at hand, and our school was no exception to this rule.

We got along without any doors for a while. The carpenters had stretched muslin tightly over the window openings so that the plastering would not dry too rapidly. This muslin served for our windows. The carpenters had also left some heavy planks and empty nail kegs in the school yard. The boys brought those into the school rooms and placed them around the walls. These we used for seats and desks. If the children were just reading they usually sat on the planks. If they were tall enough so that their feet touched the floor they were fairly comfortable; but if they were so short that their feet dangled in mid air, they offered no complaint, for these children wanted to come to school. When it was necessary for them to do written work, they put their paper on the planks, using them for a desk and sat on the floor. They did not complain about this either. They were most eager to learn. There was no nonsense, or discipline problems in these early school days. Every child seemed to feel that it was great privilege to have a school and seemed to want to do all that he could to make it a success.

Miss Bee who has charge of the primary room, has been a county superintendent in one of the smaller counties of the state. She is perfectly adorable, and entered into the spirit of the pioneering school teaching as though it was the greatest adventure of her life.

We called the children together the first day and asked them what they could bring from home in the way of books that we could use until we could get books from the County seat at Fort Pierre. They responded beautifully. They seemed to have no fear of anything about school excepting that we would not continue to have school until the building was finished. It was no wonder they were so eager for school, for there was very little for them to do to entertain themselves. In school they had the companionship of their fellows. These children seem unusually bright. Perhaps a part of that is due to their eagerness to learn, but we found only one subnormal child in the two rooms.

When we dismissed the children about noon the first day, we told them to bring paper and pencils and what books they could find at home when they came the next day, for we were going to have regular all day sessions starting the next day.

After they were gone, Miss Bee and I held a long conference making plans to carry on an informal school until things were adjusted for regular, formal procedure. We planned our reading and arithmetic to be done much as we had always done this work only we would use different texts for different children just as they were available. The history and geography we were going to direct from outlines, so that the children could use all the text books that we could find or any other suitable material. We planned to do a great deal of oral English until such a time as we had desks, so that the written work could be done with greater ease.

We outlined plans for hikes to familiarize the children and ourselves with the local geography, plant, bird and animal life. The material that we accumulated on these trips we wanted to use in our oral English work. We thought that the upper grade children might do some sketching for Art work. The school board had asked us to

"I told the school board that I could not see how any one could be expected to get along with a woman who had a chin like yours." (family photo of Tully)

make up a list of materials that we would need for the school so that they could get the order off at once.

When we had finished with all this, Miss Bee turned to me and said, "You are not a bit like I thought that you would be. I owe you an apology, for I tried to get your job after I met you at church. I told the school board that I could not see how any one could be expected to get along with a woman who had a chin like yours."

We had a hearty laugh at her frankness. I told her that nature had given me a very pronounced chin, but nature had also given me the ability to cultivate any sort of a disposition that I cared to have; and that, perhaps, determination tempered with judgment might be an asset.

We laughed again and I thanked her for her frankness and candor. Since then we have been the best of friends. In fact, I think that we have established a friendship that will last through life. She has such a keen sense of humor, a wonderful understanding of children, a good mind, and a love for the better things in literature, music and art. She is a great bird lover and has opened up a new world of enjoyment for me in the study of them.

She suggested that we should take a few of the older children some Saturday morning and hike out along the river for a study of the birds.

There were about twenty children who were interested in taking this trip. We started about five o'clock in the morning. It was still dark. Each child carried his own sandwiches; Miss Bee and I provided the cocoa and fruit, and the children brought money to buy wieners.

We had a most delightful trip which proved to be just what was needed to arouse interest in bird study. The children read every bird book that was available. Miss Bee supplemented this material from her rich knowledge.

One morning not long after our bird hike, Pete Upland who lived about a mile and a half out of town, came to school and told us that he had seen a great many cedar wax wings in a plum thicket not far from the road where it crossed the North Fork. The children were a little skeptical. One boy said, "There are no cedar wax wings in this country. How do you know that it was cedar wax wings that you saw?" Pete said, "I know them by the picture of them that I saw in the bird book. If you don't think I know what I am talking about come up there with me after school and I'll show you."

There were about twenty-five of us who went with Pete after school. He said just before we reached the thicket, "Be very quiet or you will not see them for they are very shy." We were as quiet as we could be and were well paid for our trouble for each of us was able to get a good view of the birds. Miss Bee told us the next day that these pretty birds were quite common along the Cheyenne river and no doubt they were just resting here on their migration back to their usual habitation along this river.

We were so busy studying and enjoying the things about us that the time passed rapidly until our school house was finished and our new desks installed. The man who built the school house certainly believed in exalting the teacher. At least it would appear so, for he had partitioned off a small nook not much larger than the teacher's desk. In this he has made a raised platform about eight inches high. The only black board available in either room is on the wall back of the teacher's desk.

While we were short of books and materials it was necessary to make use of this little strip of black board so often that I felt at night as though I had climbed Jacob's ladder during the day. We had a very splendid school board and they remedied all the defects about the building and provided the necessary books and materials for us just as soon as they possibly could.

Our greatest difficulty was in providing room for our ever increasing school population. The new single seats had been a great joy to these children, for many of them had used the home made desks in the log school house before the town of Philip started. Unfortunately, we soon had more children enrolled than our seats would accomodate. The school board ordered more desks promptly, but when they arrived the only way we could make room for them in the class rooms was to put two single seats together and in this way make for three children. Still this did not make room for all of them only for a short time. We used the front seats and several children sat on the rostrum step.

When the County Superintendent came to make her official visit she was horrified to find us packed in so closely. She told the school board that they must provide more room at once or she would close the school. Miss Bee and I knew that there was to be an addition built on to the school house, but we did not know just when it was to be done. Imagine how we felt when we arrived at the school one Monday morning soon after the County Superintendent's visit to find a crew of carpenters at work tearing our partitions and sawing lumber preparatory to enlarging the school house. We would have been overjoyed at this prospect if we had known it in time to take care of our school supplies, but such was not the case, and we found books, papers, pencils, water colors, scissors and what not mixed with the lath and plaster that had just been torn from the walls. We salvaged as many of the materials as we could and packed them in boxes. The men piled one box on top of the other in a corner of the room where they would be least disturbed until the building was finished. In about a week we were all back at work in our enlarged quarters.

This time I had a very large room with plenty of seats, desks and black boards. We had cloak rooms this time also. We were very happy in our new quarters, but some people were unkind enough to say that the school house now looked like a sheep shed. I like better to call it a long bungalow type of school house.

Many of the homes are just as crowded as our school house was. It is not very hard to live in a crowded condition if every one keeps well, but in cases of serious illness, it is a terrible handicap.

One family that has been sending several children to school were living in a little shack that was scarcely large enough for half that number of people, when one of the little girls, a very pretty child, with big blue eyes, and long golden curls, was stricken with spinal meningitis. Her little life was snuffed out in a twinkling. Miss Bee and I were heart broken for we were both very fond of her.

Since there was to be no school for a week or so until all danger of contagion was past, Miss Bee and I drove out to the cemetery where they were to bury her. We knew that public services were forbidden, but we followed at some distance. We were very glad afterward that we had done so, for this poor Mother came to see us as soon as she could and told us that all through the child's delirium she had called continually for Miss Bee. It seemed to have afforded the mother some comfort to know that we were with her, for she felt so alone away from her relatives and friends in her time of sorrow. Pioneering is a hard task for women and children.

The school year passed by very quickly. The children begged for a picnic for the last day. You know, Sara, I have never been very fond of picnics and I demurred a trifle, but Miss Bee was very enthusiastic

about a picnic. I am very happy that I was won over by her enthusiasm, for our picnic was a most enjoyable affair. The parents seemed
as eager for a picnic as the children were.

We chose a place down by the south fork of the Bad River for
our picnic grounds. One of the fathers fixed tables for us. The
mothers had sent word to school that they would look after the
lunch for us. They certainly did their part of the program well, for
when the tables were spread all I could think of was the basket
dinners that we used to have at camp meeting back in Kansas. There
was fried chicken, sandwiches, cake, salad, pickles and many other
good things. Miss Bee and I had ordered ice cream as our part of the
dinner, but when it was delivered that day, there was a card on it
saying that it was a treat from the school board. They, too, had
thought of giving the children ice cream for the picnic; but when
they went to order it, they were told that we had also ordered ice
cream for that day, and so they just paid for our treat.

The children had prepared a program which they gave soon after
dinner, for they were eager to go up into the road above the picnic
grounds and play games. The men and women lined up on either
side of the road and cheered for the youngsters who ran races down
between these lines. Pete Upland and Lawrence Towne were so very
evenly matched in foot racing that they tied. They had to run several
races before the men who were judges could decide which of them
won. The men became so excited over this that when Pete Upland
was finally declared the winner, his father said to Mr. Towne, "I bet
that I can beat you."

Everybody laughed for they did not think that Mr. Towne could
run a race, but he took off his shoes and surprised every one by not

only running the race, but by coming out ahead of Mr. Upland by at least a yard.

The older girls played games with the little girls so that every one had a good time. The afternoon went by so very quickly that the children did not want to go home at sundown. When some one mentioned how late it was getting the parents soon started the children toward home, but I am not at all sure, however, which ones enjoyed the day more, the children or the adults. It was the best picnic that I have ever attended.

I have enjoyed my year of teaching in this Philip school more than any other of my experience. Perhaps this is because the children have come to school because they wanted to and not because they had to.

The parents have had very few interests outside of the home, excepting the school and so they have entered into our school plans almost as eagerly as the children have. The mothers have invited Miss Bee and I into the homes until we have had a grand time. It has been pleasant to meet the parents and the children in the homes in this way.

These people are not snobbish. The town is too new to have cliques but they do have a hospitality that is unique in itself. This has been a great experience and I am most happy, Sara, to have had an opportunity to enjoy it.

Lovingly,
Tully

Odds and Ends About Things

September 15, 1909

Dear Sara:

My letters are so far apart no wonder you ask strange questions. I laughed when I read your last letter asking me why I had not told you anything about our home. Home? We haven't had a home since we came into town; we have simply had a place to stay. As I wrote you before John rented the rooms up over the drug store since that was the only available place that we could find when it was necessary for me to come into town to start school.

Since the rent for the rooms over the drug store was more than we could afford to pay from our combined salaries, we made arrangements with the hotel to rent rooms to their guests. They were to fill the rooms and collect from the people and then pay us. We were to pay the rent on the building and keep up the rooms.

Keeping up the rooms proved to be a big undertaking in addition to my school work. I had planned to keep help to do this work, but that proved very unsatisfactory.

I sent my laundry to a woman in the country who said that she needed the work. Perhaps she did. But she hung my bed linen on a barbed wire fence to dry and it kept me busy sewing up the rents in the sheets.

Market day in Philip, February 17, 1909.
(Haaken Horizons)

Our rooms were very inferior to those at the hotel so that it was necessary for us to take the guests who were satisfied with cheaper quarters.

The saloons were conveniently near. It was not an unusual thing for John to stride down the hall at night and bellow at some poor deluded soul, who had imbibed too freely of "joy water," that if he did not shut up and go to sleep that he would throw him out. This threat always worked. If you had heard John make it you would cease to wonder why it always worked.

Early in May a circus came to town. Our rooms were soon filled with the fakers who followed the show. I was not happy to be housing these people. They had come in about midnight of the night preceding the circus day. They were quiet enough that night but before the next day was over many of them had frequented the saloon too often.

One so called blind man and his woman companion were disgustingly drunk. John told them that they must vacate the room as we did not keep drunken people. The blind man said, "I'm so sorry mister, but we can't go. We can't drink all of our beer and we can't take it with us for we haven't anything to carry it in." The beer excuse did not make an appeal to John and Mr. Blindman and his lady were soon on their way.

When we went to put the room in order we found out what they meant by their beer for the water pitcher on the wash stand was almost full of beer. This experience and many others just as disagreeable made me feel that I could scarcely wait until one year was up, so that I could move out of these rooms into a house. I did not care how small or inconvenient the house might be, if it was just a place where we could be by ourselves away from this riffraff of humanity.

We were fortunate enough to get a small two-roomed house out in the west part of town. I was very happy to get this house for it was on the lot next to one that I had bought soon after I came into town.

The townsite company was offering acre tracts for one hundred dollars each. This acreage was fifty feet wide with about three hundred feet of level land. The rest of it extended back over the hill. We built a small barn near the foot of the hill leaving a lot back of that for hay. Then we fenced the rest of the rear of the lot for a place for the horses to get exercise. I had hoped to build a house on the front of the lot but our expenses have been so heavy that we have never been able to save money to do this. Therefore, I was glad to be able to get a house near the lot.

John did not seem to understand the care of the pigs that we had brought in from the farm and they soon died. This discouraged us both about trying to raise pigs so near town; but I felt sure that I could make a success of the chicken business and I had high hopes of starting on this enterprise in the early spring.

We were not able to get the little house where we were to live until the second week after school opened in September. John took Saturday off and we spent the day packing and moving out. Things were certainly in a mess. I was so tired when I crept into bed Saturday night that I said, "This has been such a dreadful ordeal that I believe if I had to move again as dearly as I love my things I would move them into the street and set a match to them."

I felt quite differently when morning came and John and I worked to such splendid advantage that by night our two little rooms were in order and we felt that we were going to be very cozy and happy there. We hated to spend Sunday doing such drudgery, but as we were both working through the week there seemed to be no other way to do it.

It was raining the next morning and the house was so dark and quiet that I did not hear John when he got up and slipped away to work very early. In fact, I was so tired from our heavy work of the past two days that I over slept. As a result I ate a light breakfast and then dressed for school.

I was surprised to find that it was raining as I was about to leave the house and back I went and changed my dress. Off came my pretty new blue suit with my hat to match. I hurriedly slipped into that old black brilliantine dress with my green cape and my summer hat.

Our school grounds were always so muddy on rainy days that a good dress would be ruined for this gumbo soil stained almost any material.

Blucher started to follow me as I left the house, but I told him that we had a home now and that his job was to stay there and watch things while I was away.

The rain soon stopped and school had only been in session a short time when a stranger came to the door and asked me to allow all the children in my room to come over to the Methodist church lot, which was near the school house, and pull on a rope that they had hitched to a plow. They were going to break the sod for a new Methodist church and wished to have a picture taken when they turned the first sod.

I was not at all sure that the school board would be willing for me to dismiss school for this purpose; but I also knew that Philip stood as a unit for anything that would boost the town. Accordingly I told my caller that if he would bring me a note signed by two members of the school board requesting me to let the children help at the church lot that I would be very glad to dismiss them.

I went back into the room, but I had scarcely started to work when there was a very vigorous knocking at the school room door. I answered the summons and I think my face must have shown my displeasure when I saw the same man standing there. I knew he had not had time to go down town to see the school officers. He said, "Step outside madam." I answered in my most dignified school ma'am manner. "Pray what for, please?" He said, "Hurry! Isn't that

The second fire in Philip, May 5, 1909.
(Haaken Horizons)

your house on fire!" I looked and sure enough there was my house wrapped in flames with the black smoke pouring from it and above it. Just as I turned around a man jumped through one of the back windows and said, "Your house is on fire, they say your dog is inside of it and I have come for you!"

Miss Bee had heard the confusion and came to see what it was all about. She said, "Go quickly! I'll look after everything here." We ran to the corner where a man was waiting with a team and buggy to take me out. There was nothing that I could do when I got there excepting to stand by and watch my things burn.

I had sold my bedding from the rooming house to a man who was going to start a rooming house in one of the new towns that had sprung up farther north. The bedding was all stacked ready for delivery and we could look between the partially burned boards and see these piles of bedding burn; also my book case with the books in it as well as the other things.

As you know, Sara, John and I have only been married three years. We have not had a house suitable for house keeping only a very small part of that time, so all my pretty wedding gifts were practically new. They were in there burning up. Oh, how I wanted to get into the house so that I could save some of them, but the house was too far gone before the fire was discovered for any one to save much. Some carpenters working about a block away broke into the kitchen and saved a few things, but they broke so many dishes after they had taken them out of the house that the fireman told them to stop, as it would be more comfort to me to know that my things had burned up than to know that they had been broken carelessly when they might have been saved.

After it was all over a very dear friend of mine had two of her grandsons bring over a small trunk and they gathered up everything into it that had been saved and took it home and stored it in their attic for me until I could decide upon what to do next.

Practically every one in town had come to the fire. There was little that one could do, yet they waited with me. It made me think of a funeral.

Miss Bee and all the children came out at noon. She said she had told some of the larger boys to come on out as soon as I left. They were so concerned about Blucher. Soon after they arrived they came to me and told me that they had found Blucher and that he was not burned. I already knew this for he came to me as soon as I arrived at the fire. I had felt no concern for him for I knew that he was not in the house when I left in the morning.

Paul and June just happened to be coming into town that morning. They saw the smoke from this fire and the big crowd of people about so they drove past to see what it was all about. They were much surprised to find out that it was our house that had burned. They took Miss Bee and me down to the hotel. When we arrived I found that my good friends there had a room ready for me. They said I was to make that my home until I decided what I wanted to do.

June and Miss Bee and I went to the room so that I could make myself presentable to go into the dining room. Things went very well until I went to powder my nose and I did not even have a powder puff. Then I sat down on the bed and nearly cried my eyes out. These were the first that I had shed, and they did not last long for I was ashamed of myself to let this trifle break my composure.

I told June what a terrible remark that I had made the night before about touching a match to my things, and that I wondered if this was a judgment sent on me for making such a wicked statement. She told me to set my mind at ease that judgment was not meted out in just that way. She said if every one received that sort of punishment for idle remarks that the world would be all topsy turvy. She dashed out and bought me a powder puff. I washed my face in cold water and with my new powder puff I soon removed the traces of my tears and went down stairs to meet my friends and to try to make my adjustment as quickly as possible without bothering other people with my troubles.

I can scarcely describe to you how you feel when you do not have anything excepting the clothes that you are wearing. Even my teaching library had burned. I felt detached from things as though I were present, but yet not a part of my surroundings. From childhood you always have some things that you can call your own. I had many keepsakes and things that were priceless to me on account of their association. These things could never be replaced.

The next evening about eight o'clock, Miss Lee, one of the proprietors of the hotel, came to my room and said that I had a caller down stairs. She said that as the parlor was being used for a sample room that evening she had asked my guest to go into the dining room. I went down, and as I opened the dining room door, I was greeted with "Surprise!" It was "surprise" sure enough and such a delightful surprise at that.

These Philip people have proven to be very good friends of mine. I often wonder if there is another group of people on earth that are so kindly disposed, unselfish and so filled with human understanding as these people are.

When the last good night had been said, I found myself the happy possessor of sheets, pillow cases, blankets, towels, stockings, dresses, gloves, underclothing and toilet articles. The last box that I opened contained an excellent clothes brush, hair brush and mirror. The note in the box read, "Brush up. Take a look at yourself. And forget it." I thought that this was very good advice for I had a comfortable place to stay, a good position and was surrounded by true friends.

No one knew how the fire started. I was sure that it was through no fault of mine, therefore, I had nothing to regret. No amount of feeling sorry about things would restore any of the articles that had been burned, and so I tried to take up life where I found it and go on as though nothing had happened.

John could not understand my view point. He felt that he had been wronged in some way, and for some reason he seemed to blame Philip. He kept saying, "If they had had a fire department, it would not have happened. If some one had told me, perhaps I could have saved something." He seemed to want to get away from Philip, but he stoutly refused to go back to Wakefield and kept talking about going back to the farm. This seemed out of the question to me for we had no money. The farm would not produce a living until it was improved and improvements cost money.

As I had friends in Fort Pierre I asked them about a job for John down there, thinking that perhaps if he got away from Philip for a while that he would come back and be satisfied. I secured the job for him all right, but when he went down to see about it he refused to go to work and came back to Philip on the next train.

The next Saturday night he told Miss Lee that it would be necessary for her to get some one to take his place as he was going back to the farm in two weeks to get things in shape so that we could live out there. Miss Lee came and talked with me to see if I could persuade John to reconsider and at least work in Philip until spring as he would not be able to do much in the way of making improvements on the farm during the winter months, but John was determined to go out to the farm right then, and he went.

Paul and June very kindly asked him to stay with them until he could get a place fixed up to live in. I stayed on in Philip to teach but I did not stay at the hotel. Miss Lee offered me a room very cheaply but I knew that she could rent it for transient trade for far more than I could afford to pay her for since John had quit work I was the sole support of our family and as yet John had not confided in me what his plans were for improving the farm. I knew, however, that what ever he did would require money and that it would be necessary for me to furnish it.

So often when the way seems very dark a bright path opens up in a direction that you least expect; and this is the experience that came to me.

Last year while we were still living over the drug store I used to make a short cut home from the school house through one of the lumber yards. One evening as I was hurrying through there on my way home from school a very pleasant faced woman stopped me and introduced herself as Mrs. Seeman. She said that they had proved up on their homestead and had built a little house about two blocks from the school house. Her husband was one of the owners of the lumber yard and they had just moved into their house in town so as to make it more convenient for him to get back and forth to his work.

She had always lived in Des Moines until they came out to the homestead. She liked the homestead and I did not wonder at that when I saw her house there after we grew to know each other better. She said that she had watched me going and coming from school for several days, and as she thought that she would like to know me she came out to introduce herself and to invite me over to her home for dinner the next evening. I went to dinner, but I stayed to visit. We had such a delightful time. I found her to be a woman with a keen mind and the ability to use it. She was well read and a most interesting conversationalist. A very warm friendship sprung up between us. Just as soon as she learned John was going back to the farm for the winter she invited me to come to her home to stay. I hesitated for some time but she and Mr. Seeman both insisted that I should come for Mrs. Seeman was lonely and she wanted me to so very much.

I can never repay these two loyal friends for this kindness for I spent the most delightful winter in their home. Mrs. Seeman was a great reader. When she found a book or a magazine article that she thought I would enjoy, I would find it waiting for me when I came home from school at night.

Often when I would come home from school too tired to enjoy conversation she would hand me a book opened to an interesting part of a story and say, "Read this while you rest," or maybe she would just tell me the story of a book or a worth while magazine article that she had read so that I found myself in a new world and one that was quite to my liking.

John bought a shack from a near neighbor. He tore it down and used this lumber with some new material that he bought down town and built a two room house. One room down stairs and one upstairs.

The weather was extremely cold that winter so that John had scarcely finished work on the house when it was time to go into the field. He planted the small field where the sod corn was last year into speltz and put oats in my garden patch. In addition to these fields he broke about five acres more adjoining the speltz field. This he planted into sod corn. He had a fairly good yield from all his crops this year.

Early in the spring I had sold my acreage near town and bought three fresh milk cows with their calves and a roan durham bull calf.

John had suggested that if I would do this that he might be able to pay for his groceries from the milk and cream. We had fenced and cross fenced the farm while we were both working in town. With our cattle in this pasture and the improvement that John had made, our place began to look like a farm, only the house looked so funny. John had made it a story and a half high but it was far too narrow for its height. It looked like a tower of some kind perched up on the hill. There was also a question as to whether it would stand against the storms and straight winds of western South Dakota.

As John did not wish to sell his grain and we had to make some provisions for storing it, I suggested putting a lean to the west side of the house. That would tend to balance the structure and later on we could finish this part up for a kitchen and dining room. John and I built this lean in two days. We thought we did very well. I helped to lay the floor and then I handed him the lumber so that he would not have to get up and down on the ladders so often. We put blue building paper over the house and the lean-to. We fastened it on with lath so that the wind could not tear if off. With this improvement and our grain stored in the bins we felt that we were ready for winter.

What of Blucher all this time? I still think that he is about the smartest dog that ever lived. He was, like John, a bit unhappy in Philip.

When we lived at the rooming house I had to keep him shut up in the room all day for the men liked to take him into those high board fence enclosures back of the saloons and have him fight with bull dogs. The poor thing would come home all so battle scarred and bleeding that it would just break my heart.

One evening as I was crossing the street with him coming from the hotel after dinner, I saw a man who owned two of the bull dogs that were Blucher's arch enemies, going up the street near where we were crossing. One dog was ahead of the man and one was trotting along behind him. Just as we were opposite our stair way, both bull dogs spied Blucher and made a rush for him. The man and I jumped out of the way, Blucher ran safely up the stairs and the two bull dogs put on a good dog fight. That is the only dog fight that I ever really enjoyed. I was not at all sorry when the men were obliged to throw several pails of water on the dogs before they could get them to stop fighting.

After our house burned down in town Blucher refused to leave the ruins, but he stayed there all the rest of the day, the first night and the second day, and was still there when John went out for him in the evening. He said that as some one might want to stage a dog fight he thought he had better bring the dog down town. But Blucher refused to leave the ruins. He would follow John for a short distance and then go back and lie down by the smoldering fire. John told me this soon after our friends left following the shower that they gave us. Then he added "Perhaps Blucher will come for you. He won't leave the lot for me." I said, "Yes, no doubt he will come with me, for I told him to stay there and watch that house, and I have never told him any differently." John and I walked out to where Blucher lay beside the ruins of the house. I said, "Come on Blucher. You do not need to stay here any longer for there is no house now for you to watch." He got up and trotted along behind me back to the hotel. He never went back to watch the ruins after that.

When John went out on the farm to live Blucher stayed with him. That was a good arrangement for both man and dog and it saved me the care of him in town.

School will soon start again. I shall be glad to be back at work. I am going to live with Miss Bee, as her sister had a position with the Western Union company at Portland. We will live in the little house where Miss Bee and her sister have lived. I think this will be a fine arrangement. I shall miss Mrs. Seeman, but Miss Bee and I are congenial companions, and I fear it would be imposing on the Seemans to go there again this year.

It seems to be rather a difficult matter to start one of these letters to you for they are written at long intervals. It also seems quite a difficult matter to stop writing for my letters are very long.

This busy life keeps my time fully occupied; for now that John is on the farm, I have much housekeeping to do there at the week ends to make him comfortable for the next week while I am away.

Lovingly,
Tully

Carrying On

My dear Sara:

I have let more than a year elapse since I wrote to you last, but last year seemed rather uneventful save for one thing, and that one thing has changed my life considerably.

Miss Bee left Philip in February and was married in June. She is now mistress in a beautiful home up on the hill overlooking Philip from the north.

I rejoice with her in her happiness. She deserves all that this world can give her and then some, for she is a beautiful character. Still I think I am filled with self pity for I am so lonely without her. There will never be anyone who can take the place she filled. We seemed to supplement each other perfectly in our work. Her strong points were my weak ones, and visa versa. Her understanding of children and the great love that she had for them brought inspiration for each new day.

She had a little rolly poly horse that she called Pansy. She left her for me to drive and I have driven back and forth to the ranch much of the time during this year. The rest of the time I have lived at the hotel. I shared Miss Lee's room with her so that I was very comfortable. Now I shall go back on the ranch for the summer.

One Saturday, when the school year was about half over, a neighbor lady who lived to the west of us came over to spend the day.

She told me, among other things, that, if she were in my place, she would always keep the doors locked, for there was a homesteader who lived not far from them who was mentally unbalanced. She said that he was apparently harmless, but that he would come to the houses and walk right in quietly and unannounced. Perhaps you would be busy and on turning around you would find this man in your kitchen. They called him the "locoed preacher." I not only felt that I wanted to keep my doors locked, but I did not feel safe in the house or about the yard. I would start at every noise I heard, expecting to find the "locoed preacher" at my elbow. The fear had taken away all the pleasure of being at home over the week ends.

John could not be around the buildings all the time that I was at home. He said he thought that I was very foolish to be so disturbed over an idle rumor, but if I was really afraid that I had better bring some girl out from town to stay with me.

I told him as I left home on Monday morning that I would bring some one home with me on Friday night as he had suggested. It was rather a cold morning and I was well bundled up for Pansy was no longer young and his swiftest pace was a dog trot. I was within about three miles of town, when I saw a well dressed man carrying a suit case walking in the road ahead of me.

He stopped as I drew near and removed the wrapping from his case and stepped to the side of the road. As I came up to him, he spoke to me and called me by name. I stopped the horse and asked him to ride into town with me. When he was seated in the buggy, he said that he had hoped that he would get a ride with me since he knew that I would be making the drive in before school. He said that, although he had not formally met me, he had seen me very often and that his wife knew me. He did not mention his name and I did not ask for it.

I found him to be a very good conversationalist. He had traveled quite extensively in the east and was able to talk most intelligently of places where he had been and of interesting people that he knew. I went out of my way to take him to the railway station for he had told me that his wife had brought him up to the forks of the road where they hoped to meet me, because his suit case was very heavy for him to carry. He said as he alighted from the buggy at the railway station, I shall tell my wife, Mrs. Dudley, that you did come along and gave me a ride the rest of the way into town. She will appreciate your kindness almost as much as I do, I am sure.

I smilingly assured him that he and his wife were both most welcome to the little service that I had rendered. For I realized now that he was no other than "the locoed preacher"; and since my fear of him had been removed, that he had rendered me a far greater service than he would ever know.

John loves to tell the story of my fear of "the locoed preacher" and then of my hauling him into town. All this could not have happened if Blucher had been alive, but I have lost Blucher. I can scarcely bear to write about it and I won't allow anyone to mention it to me. I suppose it is wrong for anyone to feel so badly over the loss of a dog. No doubt sister Anne was right when she said, "It is a blessing that he is only a dog."

Blucher and I were always pals. He took good care of me. No man was brave enough to get out of his vehicle if Blucher and I were alone, for Blucher would sit on my feet and growl and show his teeth until they would say, "Will he bite? Is he a cross dog?" Of course I would say, "Yes," and they stayed where they were. A man could have shot him if he had been so evil minded as that but since Blucher sat on my feet it might have been a bit risky. At any rate I felt safe with him about the place. He never made any fuss if John was at home; but when he and I were alone, he never left me. I had trained him from a puppy to obey conversational tones, and I enjoyed talking to him. His eyes were so intelligent that I believe that he understood all that I would say to him.

He always came into town with John on Friday afternoons when John came for me. Blucher always came directly to the basement of the church, where I taught, and knocked on the door. The children learned to know his knock and they were almost as delighted as I was to have him come.

When I would open the door in response to his knock, he would come inside and then put his paws upon my waist and make the dearest little whine. The children used to say, "That is the way Blucher says 'how-do-you-do' to you." Then he would walk up and down every aisle. I allowed him to do this, for it seemed to afford the children so much pleasure to give him a little pat, and he never offered to harm any of them. Then I would put him in the fuel room and tell him to lie down on an old sack that I kept there for his bed. He would stay there quietly until I was ready to go home.

One Friday John was unusually slow about getting started for town and Blucher grew impatient. He started off by himself several times; but John saw him in time to call him back. We had made a second crossing on Meyers' draw and another road to town so that John would not have so much snow to shovel after each storm.

John said that he forgot about Blucher for a little while, and that when he thought of him, Blucher was so far away on the new road that he either did not hear John call, or he did not want to come back. That was the last that we ever saw of him alive.

When John came to the church for me I said, "Where is Blucher?" He said, "He left home before I did and I expected to find him here." When he did not come home by noon the next day, John took a saddle horse and went out to look for him. He found him dead not so very far from home, where some one had shot him.

John fixed a box for me and we buried the little fellow down under the old willow tree where he and I used to sit and hear the old mother shrike scold at her babies.

I miss him terribly. It seems as though one member of the family were missing. John tried to comfort me by telling me that he would get me another dog. There are other dogs, of course, but there can never be but one Blucher.

It was necessary to add another room on to the school building this past year. It now looks more like a sheep shed than ever. We now have the first two years of high school. We were not expecting this added enrollment so that it was necessary for us to make some changes after school started. We housed three rooms in the school house while I took the primary children over to the Methodist Church basement. This was not very satisfactory for we were not equipped to furnish the basement for school purposes.

The school board provided some long tables for desks and we used camp chairs for seats. The tables were too high for those little kiddies and the chairs often folded up letting the youngsters down on the cement floor.

The Methodist Church of Philip under construction in 1908.
School was held in the basement.
(Photo courtesy Mrs. Fred Haberly,
First Half Century, Philip, South Dakota)

Some days it seemed to me that I spent the greater part of my time soothing the feelings and bathing the bruised heads of the children who were hurt when they tumbled out of their chairs.

One morning, Melville White, a little fellow only six years old, struck his head on the table as he fell over and then landed on his face. His nose bled so badly that I was frightened and sent for his Mother. Soon after this our new desks arrived and were properly installed on 2x4 stringers.

It seemed that when the church people rented the basement to the school district, they reserved the right to move the desks out at the week ends, so that they could use the basement for church purposes. If there was any provision in the agreement about taking good care of the school property, there was just one thing the matter with it, and that was that it didn't work. Every Monday morning when I would get to the church I would find the desks all stored in the fuel room with books, papers, pencils and crayolas in the coal bin.

They tried for sometime to heat this dark, cold basement from the furnace; but it was never intended to heat the basement, and finally the school board installed a small stove for us. We were much more comfortable after that.

John used to come for me every Friday afternoon. We were usually very late in getting started for home so that it was long after dark when we would get there. One Friday night John came for me very soon after school was out. He told me that he wished that I could come right away so that we could get started for home at once as the wind was blowing some when he came in and, if it began whipping the snow, we might have some trouble. I was ready in a few minutes and we started out of town. Just as we were pulling up the hill to the flat about two miles out of town, John said, "Mr. Jenkins and several of the men told me that I would be very foolish to start out with you on such a night as this for it looks very much like a blizzard for often the wind grows much stronger at sundown."

The wind struck us strongly in our faces as we came up the hill and John began urging the horses. They frequently broke into a run for they were eager to get home. We were within about a mile and a half of our house when it was necessary for us to cross a little draw.

As we pulled up out of this we were wrapped in a blanket of fine snow. The blizzard had struck us. John urged the horses into a run. We had to trust to their sense of direction to keep in the road, for we could not see ahead of us at all.

John shouted to me to keep close watch down by the wheel to see if I could catch any signs of the road. The wind was so cold that I felt as though I had no clothes on at all. My body was perfectly stiff from my hips up. We had a warm soap stone at our feet and were well wrapped up in blankets, but we did not dare disturb them for fear they would blow away in the wind.

We soon went down into another draw. I closed my eyes to keep the snow out of them and then I covered my nose and mouth with my mittened hand for it seemed that this fine snow would choke me.

As we came up the hill, John again urged the horses into a run. They were making some progress when our Fanny horse plunged into a freshly piled up snow drift and fell down.

John handed me the lines and told me to sit still. He spoke to the horse and then climbed out of the buggy. I could not even see him when he left the buggy, but he said the horse was lying perfectly quiet. He took hold of her head and spoke to her. She got right up without breaking a strap.

The crossing at Meyers' draw was still very bad. The banks were steep and the road leading down to the crossing was narrow and sidling and rutted. If we were to miss this road that led down to the crossing we might drive over one of the steep banks.

We were both dreading this crossing though neither of us spoke of it as we drove toward it wrapped in this blanket of snow that made it impossible for us to see even the horses, but just as we reached the brow of the hill that led to the crossing, the storm lulled enough so that we could see our way through. It struck us again harder than before it seemed, as we pulled up out of the draw but it was only a short distance to the house. We were not long in caring for the horses and getting into the house.

The storm continued the greater part of the night and our friends in Philip were greatly concerned for fear we had been lost in it.

We were lost for a short time not long after the experience I have just written about.

There was a school officers' and teachers' meeting in Philip, and I was secretary of the meeting. This necessitated giving attendance and mileage slips for each school officer and attendance slips for the teachers, so that I was busy until dark.

John grew rather impatient waiting for me, for it was snowing quite hard, and he was anxious to get started home.

We had no difficulty at all until we came up through "The Pass" near our place. All traces of the road were blotted out by the snow, and John, becoming confused in his directions, headed the horses south instead of west. They did not want to go that way. John applied the whip very vigorously and we soon pulled up at a bank so steep that the horses refused to go any further. Then John got out to investigate to see if he could find the road. He said, "We are off the road and I am sure that I do not know where we are. There is June's light but I can't see how we are to get there. You stay with the horses and I'll walk over there and then I can find my way back to the road."

I realized that he was turned around and I did not want him to start off into the rough country on foot for fear that he might get lost, or maybe not be able to find where he had left me when he got back. I finally persuaded him that it was not June's light that he was driving toward but that of a neighbor who lived to the south of us. He was so confused and so sure that I was wrong that he finally said, "Well, I suppose you won't be satisfied until we drive back up to The Pass and then investigate that other light."

We drove back up to the pass and then turned west. We had gone only a short distance when John said, "You are right. Everything has just straightened out for me and I know exactly where we are. I was surely turned around."

I remembered my experience of being lost in a storm the first year that we were in Dakota; and since my judgment on directions is usually wrong I told John that he was quite justified in losing his temper with me. I was sincerely glad, however, that for once I did not get confused in my directions.

I was glad when spring came this year for I thoroughly enjoyed the drives back and forth to town in the early morning and late evening.

It did not make a bit of difference if Pansy did jog along for there was so much to enjoy in the way of birds and flowers. Perhaps I have given the impression that western South Dakota has a bad climate made up of straight winds, thunder storms and blizzards. Of course such is not the case. When South Dakota smiles, she smiles. The weather in the spring and fall is very pleasant. The air has such a delightful tang. It makes you want to work. The days are balmy and warm and the stars at night seem near enough so that you can almost pick them from the sky.

The meadow larks are every where, also the lark bunting. They sing as they soar and whole flocks of them fly about me as I drive along. The male birds are a beautiful glosssy black with a band of white feathers across each wing. The female is about the same size, but she is dressed in a modest brown coat with a strip of white feathers across her wings.

I used to cross one draw between two large water holes. The kill-deers and snipe were always feeding along the edges of the water, while the red winged black birds nested in the cat tails that were growing just beyond the water holes.

When these warm days of spring come, we often have rain at night. If the sun comes out bright and hot the next morning, mushrooms spring up where the soil is very rich.

John and I are very fond of mushrooms. The first spring after we came to South Dakota, when it was difficult to get a variety of food, we called them "manna".

One evening as I was coming home from school, I came upon a bed of nice large mushrooms. I gathered ever so many of them, thinking John would be delighted with such a treat. When I got home June was there waiting for me to bring the mail as Paul was away at work and she was always expecting letters from him. I insisted that she should stay and have dinner with us, for I was going to have mushrooms, and I had an abundance for us all.

June stoutly refused to stay. She took her letter and hurried off home so quickly that I wondered if I could have offended her in any way.

The next evening as I came home there was a fresh supply of mushrooms in the bed so that I gathered even many more than I had the night before.

When I reached home there was June waiting for her letter. Once more I insisted that she should stay and have dinner with us for I was going to have mushrooms. She laughed and hung her head in her cute little way and said, "I believe I will. I have never tasted mushrooms, but since they did not kill you people last night, I don't mind trying them tonight."

We had a good laugh then over my thinking that I had offended her the night before.

I prevailed upon June to stay all night at our house so that we could take a hike down Meyers' draw the next morning to see the wild fruit blossoms. We started rather early and had gone only a short distance from the house when we came upon the first clump of wild plum trees. We knew that we were coming to a thicket before we could see it because the air was heavy with the perfumes of the blossoms.

We went from one fruit thicket to another for about a mile. We did not go into the small draws leading away from Meyers' draw, but they too were filled with wild fruit trees for a short distance. Some of these trees were wild plum, some choke cherry, some currant and some were buffalo berry, and the fragrance of the blossoms seemed about as strong in one thicket as in another.

The prospect of all this wild fruit made me more hopeful of making a living here. If we can do so, I am sure that I shall never want to live anywhere else.

Lovingly,
Tully

The Philip Flood

June 26, 1910

My dear Sara:

I hope that this letter coming so soon after the one that I wrote in May will not give you a shock thinking that it brings bad news. But such an unusual thing has happened that I want to tell to you about it right away.

My school work was so heavy during the last few weeks of school that Miss Lee insisted that I should stay in Philip during this very busy time. Of course I was staying with her at the hotel, but on the evening of the day before school closed just about bed time, Miss Lawrence, who was teaching in the high school came over to the hotel and asked me if I would come over and stay with her that night as her sister was away and she did not like to stay alone.

I was very glad to do this as Miss Lawrence is very clever and I never tire of hearing her tell her witty stories. She says that she enjoys hearing me laugh. She surely had plenty of enjoyment that night for she kept me in a roar of laughter until after midnight.

It seemed to me that I had been asleep only a few moments when I was awakened by the deafening roar of the rain on the tin roof on the building where we were sleeping. The ceiling to our bed room was very low so that the roar of the storm on the roof almost drowned our voices when we tried to talk. I said, "It is raining so hard that I am afraid there is a cloud burst." She said, "My greatest fear is not of a cloud burst, but how long will this old tin roof last in this storm before it starts to leak."

My fears may have been realized first, but we were conscious of hers in just a few moments for the water began to drip down on our bed.

Miss Lawrence said, "When I invited you over tonight I did not tell you that my room affords all the comforts of home but you know it now for you will be treated to a shower bath."

She got up and put the dish pan under leak number one. Then number two broke loose and so on until about all the cooking utensils in the kitchen were pressed into service catching the drip from the various leaks in the roof. After she had set out this array, I thought I could get some sleep, but about that time she decided to empty the pans for fear they would run over and damage the plastering down stairs.

The storm did not stop until about four o'clock and we had just fallen into a very heavy sleep when we were awakened by some one pounding on the front door down stairs and shouting, "Get up and get out of here as quick as you can or you will drown." I thought of those numerous pans of water sitting around the room and I began to laugh. The pounding on the front door became louder and a man's excited voice said, "Answer me! Are you awake? There is a terrible flood coming. Hurry and get up. It may be here any moment. All the ranches along North Fork are flooded and we do not know how many people have lost their lives."

We bounded out of bed when we realized that he was in earnest and we were almost dressed by the time he had finished talking.

I rushed over to the telephone in the hotel to call John to see if he was out of the path of the flood, but there was no response to my vigorous ringing. Miss Lee came in and said, "You can't get any one on the telephone. The lines are disconnected. They say that the water is up to the switch board in the telephone office right now." I said, "Then how did they hear about this flood." "Why, Mr. Wilson, your neighbor on the ranch, rode in on horseback. After he warned the people living along North Fork and spread the alarm in town, he raced back across the bridge on North Fork before the water cut him off. He said that there was a wall of water eight or ten feet high coming down North Fork that was sweeping down houses and everything that was in its path. He did not stop to tell whether any one was drowned or not, perhaps he did not know."

I rushed to the street and saw the dirty flood water coming down Railroad street. As it came around the bank corner it made me think of the head of an immense black snake. I watched it until the water came up over the side walks and began to run into the basement windows at the bank and then I was seized with unbelievable fear and I started to run up toward the hill. When I reached the printing office near the foot of the hill Mrs. Armstrong was standing in the door. She said, "Why Mrs. Graves don't run, come in here, you will be perfectly safe. We are on high ground. The water won't come up this far."

I had scarcely realized what I was doing, but her calmness brought me to my senses. She said, "You are as pale as a ghost. Come up stairs with me and I will get you a cup of hot coffee for I know that you have not had any breakfast."

Main Street in Philip flooded with water.
(**First Half Century, Philip, South Dakota**)

I had scarcely thought of breakfast up to that time, but a cup of hot coffee did taste good and I had soon collected my wits enough to feel that I should go back down to the hotel and see if I could help Miss Lee. Mrs. Armstrong said, "I am sure that you can not get back to the hotel by this time but we will go out on the porch and see." Sure enough the street was filled with water. A man was on horseback either riding or swimming his horse around in the deep water. Empty barrels and boxes were floating about like egg shells. This did not last but a short time until the water began to subside. We could not account for this but Mr. Armstrong came home about this time and told us that when the rail road company had been making some repairs on the road a year or so before that they had taken out a bridge that crossed a draw that connected North Fork with Bad river proper. They had replaced this bridge with a dirt fill. When the flood water came down the draw and struck the fill it backed up into town, but the fill was not strong enough to stand the pressure of the water and finally gave away. This let some of the water into the Bad river. The danger of a real flood in Philip was over, but all the cellars in the business district were filled with water as were those in all the houses in the west part of town. The water stood two or three feet deep in these houses for over twenty four hours. The people had taken refuge on the hill and many of them stayed all night in the new school house which had been built on one of the highest hills overlooking the town.

"A flood in Philip!" It is almost like having a flood on the Sahara Desert. The bridge across North Fork washed away and as the water was too deep to ford, it was necessary for me to stay in town until a temporary bridge could be built. As soon as it was possible to use this bridge John came for me for he had guests at home and needed a cook. It was then that I learned the particulars about the flood.

There was a terrible cloud burst up on "Dirty Woman Creek" about twenty miles above Philip. The people who lived near the head waters of that creek were sleeping in one of the summer cabins near the bank. They did not realize the intensity of the storm until they were awakened by the water lifting their tiny cabin out into the stream where it was soon broken to pieces. The mother and daughter were swept away in the flood waters, but the father clung to some of the branches in the tree tops until daylight when he was rescued by some men throwing a rope to him. These were the only lives that were lost, but the flood did much damage to many houses and other farm buildings for the uprooted trees that were carried by the flood acted as battering rams when they struck against any building that was left standing.

The flood seemed to gain in volume as it swept on toward Philip. Mr. Wilson saw the flood coming and realizing that Mr. Walker's ranch was directly in its path, he stopped there on his way to warn the people in Philip.

He found Mr. Walker and the hired men out in the corral milking. He told them about their danger. They said, "Oh, yes, we know for we have had floods before. We will have plenty of time to finish the milking before the water gets here." He told them that they would have very little use for milk if they did not get out of there right away. He then went to the house and told Mrs. Walker that she had better take the children to high ground at once for the water was almost upon them. She said, "Yes, I can hear the roar but I want to put my rugs away and pin up my good dresses so that they won't get wet for the water will probably be two or three feet deep in the house." Mr. Wilson said, "If you and Walker want to stay here and drown all right but for God's sake get your children out of here right now. I am warning you that you haven't a moment to waste. I can't wait any longer for I am going on to warn the people in town."

He put his horse into a run and started for town. The Walker's evidently were aroused by his earnestness for they started the children toward the hills and they were not far behind them.

Mr. Wilson turned to look back when he reached a high hill not far from the Walker ranch, just in time to see the water surround the house. It swayed for a moment and then settled into the flood. If the family had stayed there five minutes longer they would have all been drowned.

The Walkers went over to the Wilson home to stay until they could get temporary quarters built on their own ranch. The Wilson house would not accomodate all of both families accordingly John had taken two of the Walker boys down to our house to stay with us. It was a new experience having children in our home. For the first few days I wanted to spend all my time visiting with them. The little one was such a tiny fellow that he could not talk plain. He had never been away from his mother before and he would get so lonesome for her that he would ask to talk to her over the telephone. Who ever answered at Mr. Wilson's always pretended that they did not know who was calling for they enjoyed hearing him say, "I onts to talk to muver." Then when he would hear his mother's voice he wanted more than ever to see her. We allowed him to make the trip back and forth by himself. I would watch him until he was well up the hill then he could follow the fence the rest of the way. When he came back in the evenings he would seem fairly well contented until the next day when the performance would be repeated.

I did not know what to feed such a tiny little fellow so I called his mother to find out. She said, "Give him plenty of milk to drink and then let him have what ever he wants after that." He certainly was not hard to please for when I would ask him, "What shall we have to eat for this meal?" He always answered, "Let's have some hard boiled yeggs and some fakes."

The older boy brought his pony down to our place and he used to ride out to the fields with John so that he was seldom around the house excepting at meal times.

We had both grown very fond of the children and were dreading the time when they would leave us when an unexpected happening cut their visit short.

I telephoned to Mrs. Walker one Saturday morning asking her if I might take the boys with me that day as I was obliged to go several miles away to see about getting a man to help John with the work during the summer. I knew that I would not be back until about dark. John was going into Philip with the cream and as he had some business to attend to, would be late in getting home also. She said that Mrs. Wilson was planning on having the boys come up there that day and stay over Sunday with the family. This seemed a satisfactory arrangement for I did not care to have any one ride with me when I drove our Laura horse for while she seemed gentle, she was so high spirited that many of my friends had told me that she was not safe for a woman to drive. I was taking her on this particular trip because she was faster in the harness than any of our other horses. And I wanted to make the long trip and back the same day.

My errand was successful and I got home just about sundown. As I was passing the well on Paul's place I stopped at the watering trough to water my horse. She seemed to have difficulty in drinking with the bit in her mouth so I loosened her bridle and dropped the bit under her chin. I was standing very near the buggy but I really do not know what happened for my thoughts were with Paul and June and I was wishing that they had not proved up and gone away. It was so much more lonely without them. Without any warning and so far as I know without anything happening to frighten her, Laura jumped over the watering trough and began to run. As the buggy came past me I was caught between the front and back wheels and thrown to the ground. Since I always drive with my lines buckled together, they were dragging along and in some way they caught my left shoe and I was pulled along under the buggy. The sound of my body bumping along frightened the horse more than ever. She made a sharp turn and started up a small hill. When she did this the heel pulled off my shoe and I was freed, but I could not get up for the force of the fall had hurt my hip until it would not support my weight. I raised up on my elbow in time to see Laura stop when she got to the top of the hill and deliberately kick that buggy to pieces. I have never heard of a horse going insane, but she acted like a crazy horse. By the time she had the buggy broken to pieces she had wrecked her harness until there were just a few straps hanging to her, then she saw me lying on the ground and came dashing over toward me. Her eyes looked so big and wild that I feared that she would trample me. With a great deal of effort I was able to stand up and support myself by leaning against one of the fence posts near.

As the horse came toward me I waved my arms and shouted to her. She turned and ran directly though the fence. She scratched herself in several places but she was not badly cut. She ran off a short distance and then came back toward me. This time I talked to her quietly. She came on through the fence where she had broken it down and stood near me trembling from head to foot. Then she started to trot off in the direction of our house. I followed her as rapidly as my painful bruises would allow. When she was safely in our own place I did not bother her any further but dragged myself into the house where I layed down on the couch to wait for John. Fortunately he came very soon. He was so frightened when he looked at me and found out what had happened that he rushed to the telephone and called the doctor. He hurried out and we all felt greatly relieved when he said that although I was badly bruised that I had suffered no serious injury.

When Mrs. Walker heard of my accident she refused to allow the little boys to come back and stay with us for as she put it, "You have enough to do to take care of yourself without any children to bother with."

When I was able to go to Philip again several of my friends who had heard of my accident told me that they thought I had better trade some of my horses for an automobile. I just laughed at such a proposition but when the man who had the Ford agency came out to our house and offered to take some horses and a small cash payment for a Ford car I was very easily persuaded to make such a bargain.

It was not at all difficult to learn to drive the car for I had road sense and the mechanical part of driving a Ford is very simple. So far my greatest difficulty is getting the thing stopped when I come to a gate that is on the hill side. I have gone through two this week. One was only a three wire gate but the other one had eleven wires and I not only tore the gate all to pieces but I broke off a huge gate post. If I do not improve in this part of my driving our neighbors will not care to see me coming in my car.

I had another bad scare last Thursday night. John was detained in town until quite late. The milk cows came home about sun down and I was herding them up around the buildings for the wire gate on the corral was so tight that I could not open it.

Our house sets up on the table land above Meyers' draw but it is only about twenty feet from one of the draws very steep banks.

The first car in Philip was said to have been sometime in 1909 and
belonged to Fred Arnold. (Photo courtesy Leslie E. Fislar,
First Half Century, Philip, South Dakota*)*

When one of the cows went over near the edge of this steep bank I went over to drive her back. As I looked over the edge of it, there sat a man on horse back in the shadow just at the foot of the bank. He saw me just about the time that I saw him and he turned his horse and rode away so rapidly that he was lost from sight in a turn in the draw; almost as quickly as it takes to tell about it.

Why was he hiding down there in the shadows? Would he come back as soon as I went on the other side of the house? I had to wait for almost an hour before John came. He was as much puzzled as I was about this strange man hiding so near our house. We finally decided that perhaps he was a fugitive from justice who had been fortunate enough to catch up a gentle horse on the prairie and he was no doubt waiting for us to go down to the barn to do our chores so that he could slip into the house and get some provisions for himself.

We were more than ever convinced that this was right when one of our neighbors, Mrs. Macy and her son, Jim, came down the next morning and said they saw some man had built a camp fire down in Meyers' draw near their place the night before.

People in this western country are so hospitable that it was a very unusual thing for a stranger to camp near a house and not ask for shelter.

The Macy's were confident that the man was an escaped criminal that they stayed in the house and did not light a lamp the evening before so that he would think that there was no one at home.

This was just another prairie scare. I seem to have plenty of them.

Write to me very soon and tell me more in detail what is happening at home. Your letters seem so short compared with mine.

Much love,

Tully

Life on the Farm

August 12, 1913

Dear Sara:

Time goes by so rapidly that I did not realize that it had been years since I wrote to you. No wonder you asked me to please write in detail how we live on the farm and why my help is so necessary that I can not be spared to come to Wakefield to spend the summer.

John has never been able to make expenses on the farm. He has attributed the cause to first one thing and then another. He felt that if I could get some milk cows for him that he could make his living off from them, but the green feed only lasts here for about three months. Then the grasses dry and cure making excellent feed for beef cattle, but it does not have enough succulent material in it to make milk so that the cows that come fresh in the spring are dry by September.

It occurred to me that if we could raise alfalfa on our land that we would be able to overcome this difficulty. Accordingly year before last I had twenty acres of sod broken adjacent to the small fields that John had been cultivating. We planted this field into sod corn. The yield was very poor but the fodder served as roughage for the cattle.

~ 192

Since alfalfa seed was so very expensive we did not care to risk planting it until we were sure that the sod in our field was perfectly subdued, and so the second year we planted oats. John was late in getting the seed in the ground but it came up beautifully and the blades were seven or eight inches high and a beautiful deep, rich green when one morning in June we awakened to find the weather extremely hot and sultry. Soon the wind sprung up but it was as hot as though it came out of the oven. Our field of oats that had looked so beautifully green in the morning was seared brown before night.

We felt that this venture was a total loss for the little pasturage that this field afforded to the cattle amounted to so very little compared with the cost of the seed. I was very anxious to get this field planted into alfalfa the next spring since John could not seem to find time to disc up the soil, I hired a neighbor to get the field ready for planting.

No one had planted alfalfa in our neighborhood yet, and I wanted to be sure that I did everything that was necessary to get a good stand the first year. Accordingly I sent to the State Agricultural School at Brookings and procured enough inoculation for the quantity of seed that we planted.

I also bought a weeder with a seeder attachment so that the seed would be spread evenly.

Early one Saturday morning, John and I inoculated our alfalfa seed and began the planting of it. He drove the seeder and I followed behind with the harrow.

Poor me, I was not used to walking, to say nothing of walking on plowed ground. By night I was so tired that I could scarcely drag

A five-room brick building was constructed in 1910–1911. It had a short-lived term, burning in 1914. (Photo courtesy Mrs. Krebs, **First Half Century, Philip, South Dakota***)*

myself to the house. The next morning I awoke with a booming headache so that I was unable to get up.

John went to one of the neighbors and brought a boy back with him to drive the harrow for he felt that the seed should be covered just as soon as it was spread on the ground.

I told Miss Lee about my experience when I returned to Philip for school the next week. She gave me a good scolding and said that I let my ambition over rule my judgment. I was glad, however, that I had told her for when the experimental station at Brookings sent

Classroom in Philip's first large school house on the hill.
(First Half Century, Philip, South Dakota)

out some yellow alfalfa plants, she was able to get fifty plants for me. I was in school and would not have known anything about this distribution in time to have procured any of the plants.

Mr. Winslow, a real estate man, was going to make a drive into the country in the afternoon that Miss Lee got the plants for me and he offered to take them out to John so that he could get them in the ground right away. I wrote out very definite directions for planting them, just as the instructor had told Miss Lee and sent this out to John with the plants. I also asked him to plant them in the garden for the soil there was already for planting.

On Friday evening when I got home, I rushed down to the garden to see the alfalfa plants and imagine my surprise when I found that John had planted them all upside down. The crowns were planted in the ground with the roots sticking up in the air.

*The eight-room brick building was built in 1914 to take the place
of the one that burned. It was put in the same location.
(Photo courtesy Mrs. T. G. Thorson,*
First Half Century, Philip, South Dakota*)*

John had followed me down to the garden and stood near me
evidently awaiting my approval. I said, "Why John, didn't you understand my note? Why did you put these in the ground upside down?"
When he saw that I was in earnest he said, "I examined the plants
and thought that you did not know what you were talking about, so
I used my own judgment." He had mistaken the crown for the roots.
We hurriedly dug them up and replanted them. Since they all grew,
there was no harm done and we had many a good laugh about John's
planting the alfalfa plants upside down.

One of the young men in the neighborhood had married and moved to a homestead up on the Cheyenne river. He often stopped at our place when he made his trips back and forth to Philip for provisions. He told John that if he would come up to his place that he could have a load of cedar posts for cutting.

As we were badly in need of posts to fix up our corrals, John said that if I thought I could manage things on the farm alone for a few days, he would go with another neighbor up to the Cheyenne and bring down a load.

This seemed such a sensible thing to do that I felt sure that I could get along for a few days all right. The first day and night was uneventful, but the second evening when I went for the cows, one of them was missing. I walked along up Meyers' draw looking in every water hole to see if she could by any chance be stuck in the mud. As I came up to one large water hole I heard a low sound and sure enough, there was my pretty cow, not only stuck in the mud but her head was caught under a projection from the bank so the she was held fast. There was nothing that I could do alone. Our nearest neighbors were a mile away. I knew that the boy, Jim Macy, had a pony and I thought possibly I could get him to go for a neighbor, who lived three miles away to come with a team and pull the cow out of the hole.

I walked the mile up to my neighbors; but Jim did not want to go for help, as he was very sure that he could pull the cow out of the hole with his saddle horse. The mother readily consented to his plan. She hitched up her horse and took me home. We went down to the water hole and worked until after dark, but we could not budge the cow with the saddle horse.

I got supper for us all so that they would go directly from our house over to Mr. Larsen's to see if he would come with his team and help me. I did the milking and the other chores, and then waited for help which I was not at all sure would come.

I was much pleased to hear the roll of his wagon soon after midnight, for I thought that surely we could pull the cow out with a team of horses. We put some shovels, ropes, horse blankets, and plenty of hay in his wagon and then I walked ahead of the team with a lighted lantern so that Mr. Larsen could find the creek crossings.

We found the cow just as we had left her at sun down. It did not take Mr. Larsen long to dig away the bank and get things in readiness to pull her out but the work of actually getting her out of the hole took much longer. I drove the team as best I could while following his directions as he guided the ropes that he had fastened to her.

After many, many trials, we pulled her out on the bank. I thought that she was dead for she laid there all stretched out and did not move. Mr. Larsen said that she was not dead, but that he doubted if she lived. He helped me to fix her up as warm and comfortable as we could by piling the hay and blankets over her and around her. She was so heavy that we could not move her after we had her on the bank.

When I had paid him for his trouble and saw him start off home, I went into the house and found that it was almost three o'clock. Such a hectic night as this had been. I was not at all sure that John would come home the next day. Fortunately, for me, he did come about dark the next evening. I had made so many trips down to look after the cow that day that I was completely tired out. When John got down from his load of posts, I just stood and cried like a big baby and said, "One of the cows got stuck in a water hole, and I am so tired."

A rancher friend came past the cow early the next morning. He rode up to the house and told John that he had a large stone boat that he would bring over so that we could move the cow up to the corral where we could take care of her.

He and two of his men came back in an hour or so with the stone boat. They helped John get the cow moved into the corral, but all of our efforts to save her were useless. She died in about two weeks. As she was one of our best milk cows, her death meant quite a loss to us, and in our desire to get a start in cattle, we had not counted on any losses.

As Jim Macy and his mother and I were on our way down to the water hole on the night that the cow was mired there, we passed Bill Smith's shack which has been unoccupied since he had left South Dakota.

Jim said, "I think I shall come down here and set some traps under that shack for I believe there are skunks under it." Within a few days he did come down and set them there. He had quite a line of traps set under deserted shacks and was making his spending money from the hides of the skunks that he caught.

A day or so afterwards he rode up to the door and asked if I would go over and help him with his traps. He said that he had a big skunk caught in the trap but he was so far under the shack that he could not see to shoot him. I told him that as and his mother had been so kind as to help me when I needed help, that I would gladly go with him, but that I was terribly afraid of skunks. He assured me that I would not be near this one and probably would not even see it. He just wanted me to pull on the wire that held the trap so that he could get the skunk far enough out into the light so that he could see to shoot it.

The skunk was so heavy or he had caught the wire on something; at least it took both of us to pull him. We thought that we had moved him a short distance. Jim said, "I'll hold on to the wire, while you look under the house to see if you can see him." The child apparently lost his head, for just as I stooped down to look under the house, he shot. The bullet just missed my head. He dispatched the skunk with his next shot, but I did not go skunk hunting with him again.

As I missed Blucher so very much I thought that I never wanted another dog on the place, for no other dog could possibly take his place; so that when John came home from Philip one night with a dog that looked much like a coyote, and said, "I have brought you a new dog. What are you going to name him?" I said, "Suppose you have this dog for yours, and you name him what ever you like." He said, "All right, I shall call him Jack."

Jack has an intelligent look in his eyes, but he will not do anything that he is told to do. When you speak to him, he gets up and wags his tail and seems to want to please you, but he does not mind you.

John said he thought that the dog did not have good sense, and that he would take him back to town. I suggested that perhaps the dog had been trained by a foreigner and did not understand English.

We have never allowed our calves to run with their mothers for we milked the cows; but we have always brought the calves into a calf pen at night to be fed.

Jack made a great deal of trouble for us by cutting the calves back when we would get them almost into the calf pen. Sometime he would run them for a half a mile before he would stop. It was useless to shout at him, for he only ran faster and barked louder than ever.

One evening when I came home from town John said, "Well, at last I have found out how to make Jack stop running the calves. I just shout, 'Damn you!' and he drops right where he is." I said, "Why John, how did you ever happen to make such a discovery!"

He closed the door quickly and went out to the barn, leaving me to draw my own conclusions.

A few days after this, John went into town; and as he had not yet come home when it was time to bring the cows in, I took the dog and went after them. It was an easy matter to get the cows in; but when it came to getting the calves, that was quite a different matter. I would get them almost up to the calf pen when Jack would cut them back. He worked as hard as I did, but we were not making much progress toward getting the calves in the pen.

I lost my temper and was berating the dog on his stupidity, when I happened to remember what John had said about swearing at him. By this time I was about a quarter of a mile from the house and down in the creek bed near where the road crossed. I thought I was perfectly safe from human ears and eyes so I shrieked at the dog, "Damn you, stop!" He dropped down to the ground as though I had struck him. I heard a noise and looked around. There was an automobile from town filled with men that I knew. They had slowed down for the crossing and had heard what I said. They had a hearty laugh at my expense. After this, I was able to get the calves into the pen without any interference from the dog.

John and I decided upon certain commands that we would use with him. He learned these very readily and has proved to a valuable dog.

I had a chance to get twenty pigs from a neighbor who was selling out and leaving the country. We had plenty of skimmed milk by this time for we were milking about twenty cows. I bought the pigs and hauled water for them all summer, from a water hole down on Meyers' draw. I would hitch "Old Dan, the broncho," up to a stone boat and drive down to the water hole. I had to dip the water up with a pail. This proved to be almost more than I bargained for before the summer was over, for pigs needed so much water that I often thought my back would break before I had my fifty gallons of water dipped up and poured into the barrels on the stone boat. Maybe you don't what I mean by a stone boat, Sara. I had never heard of them until I came into this country. It is something like a sled with poles for the runners so that the sled rides low on the ground. The heavy planks that are nailed from one runner to the other makes the sled strong enough to carry heavy loads. I suppose perhaps that it was originally used for hauling stone is how it gets the name of stone boat. I thought when I first heard the men talking about one that they meant a boat made out of stone.

It seemed that we would never get enough land under cultivation to make our farm pay expenses if we waited to break the sod by horse power. I had a chance to get a steam tractor to come in and break fifty acres for me and that seemed the best and quickest way to get it done.

We planted this to sod corn the first year; but we were so late in getting planted that the hot winds caught it when it was about a foot high, so that it did not even make fodder.

John said that if I would buy the seed wheat, that he would plant this field to winter wheat in October. I bought the seed but John could not seem to get the planting done. I finally hired a man to come and plant it, but by this time it was so late that most of it winter killed.

We heard a great deal about dry farming these days. Some speakers went so far as to say that there would be no crop failures, if the crop was properly cared for and the dust mulch kept over the soil.

I told John that I would buy the seed and cultivate the corn if he would plant twenty-five acres for me, so that I could have it to feed to my pigs. We were able to get some good seed corn, Minnesota Number 13. John planted the field late in May just ahead of a heavy rain. This was followed by good growing weather, so that by the time I was out of school, the corn was ready for me to cultivate. We had a riding cultivator and I was very proud of myself when I had finished cultivating the field for the fifth time.

The corn grew very rapidly and was tasseling out in fine shape when a hot wind came up one day and seared it. The wind blew for three days and at the end of that time, the corn in the field was scarcely fit for fodder. I took the mower and cut it down. John piled it up to use for winter fodder for the cattle.

My dream of making money from my pigs was over. We sold them for a very little more than I had paid for them and I had all my hard work of hauling water for nothing.

I was so discouraged after this experience that I begged John to sell out and go somewhere else. I felt that if we could buy five acres of land we could raise chickens enough to make more money than we were making here. John said, "Why don't you try raising more chickens here. You have not tried that yet."

I told Miss Lee about my experience with the pigs and what John had said about the chickens. She said, "If you want to raise some chickens on shares, I'll get two dozen buff rock hens and will pay half of the feed bill. Then we can share fifty fifty on the eggs and chickens.

I bought an incubator the next spring and some Rhode Island Red eggs for it. This worked fine. We had hatched out about three hundred chickens. The weather was getting so warm by this time that we thought that it would be best to put the incubator in the cellar. One night about midnight when it was about time for the eggs in the incubator to hatch, I was awakened with the smell of smoke. I got up quickly and went downstairs and opened the cellar door. There I encountered a perfect wall of smoke. I called to John to hurry for the house was on fire. He came bounding down stairs, snatched a pail of water that was in the sink and dashed down the stairs into the cellar. The smoke was so dense that it took him a few moments to find the incubator for he had sensed at once that it was the incubator that was making the trouble.

He found that the damper that controlled the lamp had fallen down over the top of the chimney completely closing it. The chimney had filled with soot causing all the smoke to come out into the room.

John was able to find the lamp and blow out the light. We were indeed grateful that the smoke had awakened me in time to prevent a fire. Of course, the eggs in this incubator were spoiled but since I already had about three hundred little chickens, we decided not to set it again. It was too hot by this time to keep the incubator any place but in the cellar, and were afraid to keep it there after this experience.

I discovered long before the summer was over that you not only "can't count your chickens before they are hatched," but neither can you eat them before they are large enough.

I think the coyotes must have held a convention and passed the word along that I had three hundred baby chicks that would soon make fine eating for them for try as hard as I might, the coyotes would win every time. They grew so bold that they came right up into the yards and took them.

One morning I fed the chickens near the barn where we were milking. I soon heard a great commotion among them. We looked out in time to see a coyote running off with a chicken in its mouth. John kept a gun in the barn to keep the hawks away from the chickens. He snatched his gun and shot at the coyote. He did not hit him but he frightened him so badly that he dropped his prize. We ran over to where it was and to our surprise, we found that he had two chickens instead of one.

Either through bad luck or bad management on my part, my chicken venture was a dismal failure for I was able to raise only thirty of my three hundred chickens.

The coyotes would carry them off into the brakes to the south of us. It was not an unusual thing when we were hunting for the cattle to find some fresh red feather where some coyote had enjoyed a recent feast.

I did not have any better luck with my turkeys. They would hide their nests out and that made them easy prey for the coyotes. It was very discouraging to find the nest and the feathers of a turkey for you know that you had been outwitted as Mr. Coyote had found the nest first. We did raise one fine turkey gobbler which we were planning on having for Thanksgiving dinner. He roosted high on a pole on the barn. Two nights before Thanksgiving, he disappeared. I have never felt very sure of his fate, but at any rate, we did not have him for Thanksgiving.

Hog raising and chicken raising seems to be out of my line. I think I shall confine my energies to my school teaching. I am going to teach a rural school this next year. It is only three miles from home. John feels that he can get along much better with his work if I am at home to help mornings and evenings.

The children in this little school are very bright. I shall be very happy to see how much I can accomplish when I have fewer children to work with. The rural school board has very generously offered me the same salary that I was getting in Philip. I shall drive back and forth from home every day.

With all the experiences that I have had in school teaching, this little school should prove a joy and a delight.

Lovingly,
Tully

The Indians As I Know Them

October 5, 1918

My dear Sara:

You have asked me several times to tell you about these Sioux Indians. You seem to think that they are still blood thirsty and that some warrior brave may be wearing my scalp at his belt some of these days.

Your fears are quite groundless, I assure you. We are living on a part of the Sioux reservation, but the Indians never cause the white people any trouble these days. They are controlled partly through kindness and partly through fear.

They are confined on reservations where they are under the care of the government officials who give them the rations that the government provides, and grants them their leaves of absence from the reservations.

Many of these Indians have quite a number of horses. When they make their pilgrimages to visit friends in other tribes, or when a number of them come into town, they have out riders who drive a number of horses after the wagon caravan.

It is easy to tell a string of Indian wagons from ordinary travelers for many of them have bows on the wagons for a canvas covering, but you seldom see an Indian riding in a covered wagon. The old buck sits up in the spring seat while the squaws and the children sit flat on the floor of the wagon bed back of him.

These caravans used to go through our horse pasture very often. They seldom, if ever, closed the gates, which caused some one several hours of riding to find our colts if we did not see the Indians going through in time to close the gates to keep the colts in. One day I saw a long caravan of Indian wagons pull into our pasture and stop. Soon I could see the Indians running about. They would stoop down as though they were gathering fuel, then they would scatter out over the hill side.

I called John's attention to them. He said he had never seen them act so queerly before. He watched them for a moment and then his curiosity got the better of him, and getting his saddle horse he rode over to see what they were doing. He made for his excuse that he had come over to see if they had closed the gate. He found Indians digging Indian turnips as they called them. We called them wild onions. They were laughing and having a fine time. John said they seemed as pleased as a group of children over their find.

They stayed in the pasture for several hours. In fact, we had quite forgotten about them when John said, "I guess I had better ride over to the east pasture gate and see if those Indians closed it. He found the gate open as usual for our red skinned friends do not assume any feeling of responsibility whatever. As John was closing the gate he noticed some obstruction on the road just at the top of the hill. He rode up to see what it was and found that the Indians had driven two forked sticks in the ground, one on either side of the road, and had layed a pole across the road resting it in the forks of these sticks. This road was rutted and sideling. In fact the ruts were so deep on the down hill side that I always felt relieved when we were safely up and down it. Whether our Indian friends had some accident here, we never knew, but they certainly felt that this road should be closed. They never bothered us after this by going through our pasture. They always took the road to the north of us. They liked to be away from the reservation and often made trips over to the Rosebud Reservation to visit their friends there.

As their children attended the Indian school at Rapid City, it was always necessary for them to make two trips a year down to Philip to bring the children into town in the fall and come for them in the spring. These children hated to leave home as badly as the parents hated to have them go away. It was not an unusual thing for these homesick boys and girls to run away from school and start back for the reservation.

The peace officers from the various towns go in search of them, so that it is almost impossible for them to reach the reservation before they are overtaken and sent back to school.

Since time is of no object to an Indian, they made these trips extend over as many weeks as the officials would grant them leave of absence from the reservation.

When they were in Philip they would either camp close to the hills or near the river.

John and I drove past their camp one evening just about dark. There were several big fat Indian bucks and squaws sitting near a camp fire watching some very small Indian boys run foot races on the other side of the camp fire.

When a race was finished they would all laugh very heartily. Some of the squaws would clap their hands, perhaps they were imitating the whites, but the bucks sat with their arms folded and shook their fat sides and laughed until they became conscious that we were watching them. They gave a few grunts and everything grew quiet. John and I drove away hoping that we had not completely spoiled their evening.

The Indians like celebrations. They come to town in large numbers for the Fourth of July, County Fair or any other celebration that Philip stages.

They dress themselves up in buckskin, beads and feathers and lend a very colorful atmosphere to the occasion.

Occasionally the men about town get them to pow-wow. This was most interesting to me when I first saw it.

While we were living over the drug store in Philip, John came rushing up stairs one evening telling me to hurry and come with him as the Indians were going to pow-wow down by the depot.

When we arrived, we found the Indians dressed in buck skin, beads, feathers and paint, carrying their beaded war clubs and tomahawks. The squaws and the older men had their straight black hair braided in two braids down their backs. Some of them had the ends of the braids tied with bright colored ribbon. Others had the ends of the two braids tied together.

The Indians formed in a large circle, the squaws and fat men folded their arms and stood close together in the circle. They all made a queer, chanting noise like ki, yi, ki, yi, all the time the circle was moving around toward the left, each person taking very short side steps.

The young men, however were much more active. They ran around the inside of the circle partially bent double, then they straightened up and threw their heads back and patted their hands

*Charle Medecine Boy. (*Haaken Horizons*)*

"Indian War Dance" on Main Street in Philip.
(Haaken Horizons)

over their mouths, while they emitted the most frightful howls. They more nearly resembled a coyote's howl than anything else that I can find for comparison.

The white men from the outside of the circle were tossing money into the ring. The Indians scrambled for it and then continued their performance. The young men seemed to think that the more hideous they looked, and the more unearthly noises they made, the more likely the white men would be to give them money.

As the Indians are too excitable to continue this sort of thing very long with safety to all concerned, the officials soon broke up the pow-wow and the Indians were sent back to their camp.

One evening as John was riding after the cows, he saw a caravan of Indians coming. When he drew near to them, the Indian in the first wagon stopped his team and motioned for John to ride up near to the wagon.

When John was within speaking distance of the Indian he pointed toward our house in the distance and said, "Your tepee?" John said, "Yes." "Heap wallah, tepee?" the Indian asked. John knowing that I was at the house alone and that I would be terribly frightened if this Indian caravan should come there just at night, said, "No, no, little water tepee, water no good."

The old Indian threw out his chest and slapped three times and said, "Ogallalah me! Ogallalah me!"

He was no other than Chief Ogallalah! When John came back and told me of his meeting with Ogallalah and this tribesmen, I said, "Well you were not wrong about the water, for all that we had was the rain water in the cistern and it tasted so strong of the cement that it was far from good."

Miss Lee used to teach in an Indian school. When the ranch women who had lived in this western country for some time used to come into the hotel, they would often spend the evening in the exchange of experiences that they had had with the Indians.

I often told Miss Lee when we would get up to our room at night that I was so afraid of an Indian that I would not know what to do if one should ever come to our place when I was alone.

She always assured me that an Indian would not harm me if I gave him food and was kind to him and did not act as though I were afraid to him.

The frost had come unusually early on this particular fall and found us far from ready for it. John had just started to cut the corn for fodder. It had not matured enough to husk and put in a bin. As the winds soon stripped the frosted corn leaves from the stock, we could not wait to cut the corn by hand. A friend who lived several miles the other side of Philip was kind enough to bring his corn binder and come over and cut our corn for us.

The men were changing horses every half day so that they could work them harder while they were in the harness and, too, by changing men and horses they could put in longer hours and perhaps in this way they could save all of the feed.

John had asked me to go around the fence in a forty acre pasture that was near the house to see if the fence was in good repair so that they could put some of the horses in there where they would be easy to catch.

I had done three sides of the fence and was coming up on to the hill on the fourth side when I saw a horseback rider coming across the fields toward our place. I hurried back. Just as I entered the back door I heard a vigorous knocking on the front door. When I opened it, there stood a much dreaded Indian visitor, a young man, I should say in his late twenties.

He said in rather a whining voice, "Indian all wet, Indian all cold, Indian want white woman let Indian come in get warm."

It was rather a chilly, damp morning and I could readily see that he might be damp and cold, but the only fire I had was the range fire in the kitchen, and as it was necessary for me to start dinner right then, I said, "Well, come on out into the kitchen. I have a good fire out there, and it will only take you a few minutes to get warm." I opened the oven door and placed a chair in front of it for him and went on about my work, trying to remember what Miss Lee had said that if I treated an Indian all right that I would have no reason to fear him.

I tried to keep my eyes on my strange guest as I went about my work. I soon saw him nod and knew that he was asleep. When it was necessary for me to pass near to his chair, I detected the odor of whiskey and realized for the first time that I had admitted a drunken Indian. My moving about the kitchen seemed to disturb him and he became talkative. He told me that he was a graduate of the Carlysle Indian school, but that he had come back to his people after finishing school and now had sixty-five head of horses of his own on the reservation. He tried to trade me the horse that he was riding for a saddle horse that we had in the barn. I remembered the experience that I had with the drunken man at the hotel in Philip, who thought he owned the railroad. So I told him that the horse he saw was a plow horse and that we could not spare him from the field work.

Next he wrote a name on a piece of paper and handed it to me, saying, "You know her?" When I looked at it, I saw that it was the name of a neighbor girl who lived a few miles to the west of us. Her parents were foreigners and this girl helped about the farm as though she were a man. She had worked out in the sun until her skin was tanned and she looked more like an Indian than a white girl.

John and I often spoke of her devotion to her parents and her untiring efforts to do all that she could to make their lives pleasant for them. Her sister worked as a domestic in Sioux Falls. Lena never left her parents but only to go about the farm at her work. When they went to town she went with them.

You can imagine my surprise when he said, "I want you, I want your man, help Indian get her for my squaw."

About this time it was necessary for me to get something from my pantry shelves. These were in the stairway leading down to the cellar. As I opened the door, Mr. Indian raised up out of his chair and peered into the cellar way. He said, "Are you white woman? Are you alone?"

I said, "Yes, of course I am a white woman, but I am not alone. There are plenty of men about the place. Didn't you see that one coming in with his teams from the south field and my husband coming with the horses from the pasture that you came through. They are down at the barn now and will be up here for dinner in a minute."

The truth of the matter was that the man in the south field would not come in for his dinner until John ate his dinner and took some fresh horses out to work on the corn binder.

John had ridden out to catch up these horses. Sometimes it took him a long time to catch the horses, while at other times he would get back in a few minutes. Since he had already been gone for some time, I feared that he was having trouble in finding the horses and that he might be gone for sometime yet. Fortunately for my peace of mind, as I looked out of the window I saw John drive the horses into the corral at the barn, jump off from his saddle horse and tie him to the hay rack and start for the house.

He came directly into the kitchen. The odor of whiskey was so strong in the room that he took in the situation at a glance. He said, "Hey fellow, what are you doing here? I think that you had better move on."

I remembered what Miss Lee had said about feeding the Indians, and I insisted upon preparing a plate of warm food for him from my freshly cooked dinner, for I did not care for him to harbor any ill feeling and make a return trip to even up an old score. He sat down at the table and minced at his food for a few moments while John sat near by glowering at him.

They soon left the room and I was greatly relieved when I saw the Indian ride away.

John came into the house and said, "Don't you ever let a drunken Indian in this house again. What if I had not come home, how would you have been able to get rid of him?" I said, "Don't worry, I will never let any Indians in the house again for I did not know that one was drunk until after he was in here."

Our neighbor girl Lena did not fare as well. It seems that when an Indian wants a girl for his squaw, he either puts a blanket around her, or he ropes her.

This Indian had ridden up to where Lena and her father were at work on two or three occasions but they had not thought anything of his doing so.

One day she was out herding the cattle near a shack on a piece of land that they had rented. The people who had homesteaded the land had left many magazines in the shack when they proved up and gone away. They had told Lena to go into the shack and read anytime that she cared to. On this particular day, she was seated on the floor reading when she saw a shadow pass by the window. She jumped up but before she could get outside, the Indian had roped her.

She screamed until her father heard her and came running over. The Indian jumped on his horse and rode away, but poor Lena could not over come her fear. That evening the father came over and asked John to go for the doctor. He told John what had happened and said that as they had not been able to quiet her, they felt that they should have the doctor come out. The doctor thought that she had a form of hysteria caused from the shock and the fright. He said that with proper rest and quiet that she would probably be all right in a few days. Unfortunately, poor Lena never recovered. She developed melancholia and became hopelessly insane.

It may be all right to rope an Indian girl as a method of wooing, but it does not work so well with the white girls.

The Indians here are picturesque and the people who know them well manifest great interest in them and seem to feel only kindness and sympathy for them.

Conditions on the farm are better. I am sure that our corn fodder will provide plenty of feed for our stock this winter and that gives us a feeling of security for another year.

Much love,
Tully

Our Part in the War

April 30, 1919

My dear Sara:

At last this awful war has come to a close. You have been so placed that you were in the thick of things and I expect you often wonder what we people who are in these out of the way places found to do to help.

When the war started in Europe in 1914, we felt as many other people did, that the United States could never become embroiled in it.

Yet when we did enter, of course we tried to do our part as all other loyal American citizens. There seemed to be plenty for all of us to do regardless of where we lived.

Since John was too old for active service, we tried to help by putting in more wheat, milking more cows, and raising more garden. I canned all the meat and vegetables that I thought we could use during the winter. We mixed all the cereals together that we were allowed to buy and I made bread from the conglomeration. It was far from good. That coarse stuff may be good for some people's stomachs, but it very nearly wrecked mine. Since I carried cold lunches with me to school I was obliged to use this terrible bread for sandwiches. That is a mere trifle to fuss about when our nation has been so torn by this awful strife.

John was unable to do the work on the farm alone before we tried to do an extra amount as our share to help with the war. For a short time after we entered, it was not difficult to get young men to work on the farms, but as prices soared in everything, we were unable to pay the wages demanded by this labor. That did not make much difference for it was only a short time until there was no such labor available. There seemed to be only one other thing left to do and that was to take in a partner, which we did. We got a young man with a wife and children.

As soon as stock and farm produce began to bring high prices we got the land fever along with every one else in the farming communities. We bought two quarter sections of land to the south of us. One of these had a fairly good sized four room house on it. We moved this up in front of our house and put a new roof over both of them. We planned for both families in the partnership to live together. As I would be away at school every day and John out to work, we thought this would be the cheapest and best way for us to solve our housing question. It worked out as this sort of thing usually does, that "A very small house for one family will do, but there never was a house that was big enough for two."

We dissolved the partnership soon after the Armistice was signed and I am sure that both parties were glad to have it that way.

It wrung my heart during the enlistment to have my school boys starting off for war. We often drove into town in the evenings when we knew that several of them were leaving on the night train.

One night just as the train pulled out, I was standing in a dark a corner of the station crying when one of my friends came up to me and said, "Mrs. Graves, why do you care like this. None of these boys are your sons. You have no boys to go to war." I said, "My dear lady, that is just where you are mistaken. I have more boys in the service from this community than any other woman, for I have been a 'School mother' to most of them who have enlisted."

Then came the draft and Philip continually sent out its quota of young men until it seemed that there were no more left to go and some of the older men were being held in readiness, when the Armistice was signed.

I suppose our little community did not differ greatly from any of the other small farming communities scattered over our beloved America.

"What did we women folks do?" Oh, just the same as all of you other women. We worked for the Red Cross and sold Liberty Bonds. When John was having such great difficulty in

The soldier pictured is Thorval Thorson, life long resident of Haaken county. Like many of the others in World War I, he served in France. Haaken county had 375 men registered for the draft in 1917. (First Half Century, Philip, South Dakota)

getting his farm work done, he said, "If you were at home night and morning to help with the work perhaps I could get along as other men do."

Accordingly I gave up my position in the Philip schools and planned to stay at home for a year to see if we could be successful farmers by both of us working at home.

When the school officers in this district, where I am teaching, heard that I was not going back to town to teach the next year, they offered me this little school for the same money that I was getting in town. John and I both felt that we could not afford to turn this proposition down and I have been teaching here for two years so that I could come home every day. I was very glad to be living at home during the war, for this gave me an opportunity to mingle with my neighbors more freely and to learn to know them better than I had ever been able to do in all the years that I had taught in Philip. Mrs. Dorcas had charge of the Red Cross sewing for our township. We would meet to sew on Saturday so that all of us could attend the meetings. Some of us who had cars would take those who had no way of getting to the meetings and we usually had perfect attendance.

We held these meetings in the different homes. Sometimes one hostess would furnish the lunch, but more often our entertainment committee notified us what we were to prepare for the lunch. On these occasions our lunch was in the nature of a picnic so that our hostess could give her time to the Red Cross sewing the same as her guests did. Although I am not very clever at garment making, I do enjoy making button holes and I took that as my part of the work. The other ladies were very willing to excuse me from any other part of the sewing if I were willing to make all the button holes. I kept up my part of the work fairly well but I was obliged to take home many garments and often worked late at night so that I would not cause the delay in a shipment of clothing.

In addition to the sewing, I had charge of the knitting for our township. I used to bring quantities of yarn out from town and I would send this by the school children to the various women who needed it. They in turn would send back the knitted articles and I would take them in to the Red Cross headquarters in Philip.

I knew very little about knitting when we started this work, but it was not at all difficult to learn. Some of the women always had trouble in making the toes and heels in the socks. When they would get a pair of socks that far along, they would send them over for me to finish them. I learned to knit without looking at my work and did a great deal of it in the school room as I walked about at my school work. I wore an apron with a very large pocket where I kept my ball of yarn all the time. If I needed to use my hands to help the children about their work, I would drop knitting, needles and all into my pocket until I was ready to use it again.

The school children became much interested in my knitting and they were eager to learn to make sweaters for the soldiers. I told them that I would teach them how to knit if they would bring knitting needles from home.

Knitting a sweater was quite an undertaking for little boys from ten to thirteen years of age but they were very patriotic and sat and knitted like little old women. Each one of them finished a fairly good looking sweater. They wanted to undertake knitting socks, but the war was over before they learned how to do this.

The little folks whose hands were too small to hold the big sweaters knitted wash cloths. I really think that a wash cloth from them was about as much of a contribution as a sweater from one of the older children.

I was appointed to sell the Liberty Bonds in our township. This was not a hard task for our citizens were all very loyal but it necessitated my making long drives after school was out in the evening as I had no other time to call at the various homes.

I had been on one of these long drives in the early spring. The roads were so muddy that I did not take the car for fear of getting stuck in the mud. I drove old Dan, our broncho horse. He was so slow that it was almost sun down when I came to the gate that led into our place. John was there on horseback waiting for me. He said that the warm wind that day had brought down so much water and ice that I could not get across Meyers' draw near home, but would be obliged to cross on a fill that was on the highway about a half a mile north of our house. He rode along with me until we came to the place where I was to cross the draw. The water and ice had caved the fill out in places until there was just room enough for the buggy to pass. Large cakes of ice were on the crossing and the water was running across the road.

Old Dan took one look at all this then he snorted and started to back up. John said, "Whip him, whip him and make him cross!" I took out the whip and applied it as vigorously as I could but old Dan paid no attention to this lashing whatever. He continued to back up until he had the buggy cramped and right at the edge of the roaring torrent of water and ice.

John jumped off his horse and came to my rescue when he saw that I was unable to manage old Dan. He took him by the head and led him around so that he could not see the water and then he tied his saddle horse back of the buggy and took the lines and whip. I said, "Oh, please let me out of the buggy. I can't ride across there with this awful broncho." He said, "Now, just how do you think that you are going to get across this creek? You won't ride horseback and surely you do not think for one minute that you can wade across here in this swift water filled with cakes of ice."

Of course I knew that I could not wade this swollen stream but I was panic stricken to think of having to ride across behind that broncho.

John applied the whip so vigorously that old Dan once more came to the water's edge but no amount of hammering would make him step into the water.

John said, "I'll ride my horse across and lead him. Probably he will not be afraid if the other horse crossed just ahead of him." This plan worked although the old horse stepped very gingerly into the deep water and stopped several times to snort on the way over, we reached the other side safely. We had to go a long ways around to get through the gates that led down into our lane and it was after dark when we got home. There was still supper to get and all the chores to be done. I told John when we were getting to bed about midnight that I guessed we had really rendered service for our country that day.

As soon as the epidemic of the flu broke out in the winter of 1917, I telephoned to one of the doctors in Philip and offered my services as a nurse. He said, "Oh, Mrs. Graves, I need some one who is not taking care of flu patients to take care of the baby cases for me. I wish you would hold yourself in readiness to do this kind of work."

I said, "But Doctor, I have never helped a baby into the world in my life and I am not at all sure that I can do that sort of nursing."

He answered very abruptly, "If I did not think that you could do it all right, I would not ask you to. I'll expect you to be ready to go whenever I send for you." Then he hung up the receiver and I knew that my work was mapped out for me for some time.

One morning soon after this, our phone rang so vigorously about three o'clock that I ran to answer it only to find that it was one of our neighbors calling. Her daughter was very ill and they wanted me to come right over. I dressed as quickly as I could and told John to go on back to sleep for I would take the car and drive over by myself then I would have it so that I could come home whenever I was through.

I will admit that I was a bit nervous as I drove away in the darkness on this strange, new mission, for I had a foreboding that everything might not be all right. This new responsibility seemed rather heavy in addition to all the duties that I had assumed as my part of the war work.

The doctor was waiting when I arrived, but the young, seven pound daughter did not put in her appearance for several hours later.

The young mother was as brave as any woman could ever be. She bore her long hours of suffering without a complaint but when she looked at her new baby she said, "Wouldn't it be grand if my husband could see her now." Her boy husband was over seas in France. She did not know just where. He never saw his daughter for she only lived a few days. Again the young Mother was as brave as any soldier. No doubt her anxiety for the living overshadowed her grief for the dead, for our boys in France were on the battle front at that time.

About two weeks after this we heard that another baby girl had arrived at the Downey home. These neighbors lived about five miles northeast of us.

The next morning after we heard this news, a car drove into our place about five o'clock in the morning and we heard Mr. Downey's voice call, "Are you up?"

We dressed hurriedly and went down stairs. He said, "Our baby has cried since yesterday afternoon. My mother-in-law has given out completely and my wife is up trying to quiet the baby. We were unable to get hold of the doctor all night as he was out caring for the flu patients. He has all the work to do alone now for the other doctor has the flu. They say that Doctor Smith goes from house to house for there is some one very sick in every house. People know that he will do this and it saves his time and energy in making extra trips. There are so many people seriously ill in Philip right now that he can not be spared to make a trip into the country. He told me to come for you that you knew how to take care of babies."

I assumed that the baby had the flu, accordingly I took my flu mask and plenty of disinfectant as the doctor had directed me. When we drove up in Mr. Downey's yard we could hear the baby crying. The father said, "I surely hope that you can quiet her for she won't live much longer if you can't, and my wife won't be able to stand the strain either."

I went into the kitchen and put some disinfectant on the stove in hot water so that the fumes would permeate the house. There was a good fire so that I was soon warm enough to go to the sick room. I took the precaution of putting on my mask, but I soon removed it when I got inside for neither the baby or the mother had the flu.

I found the new mother seated in a rocking chair holding the baby. Both of them were crying and so was the grandmother. I took the baby from the mother's arms and gave it to the grandmother while I helped the mother back to bed.

When I had prepared a dish of warm olive oil and put some warm water in a cup and heated a fresh blanket, then I took the baby in my arms. She had cried incessantly ever since I had been in the house. The grandmother said as she handed to me, "She has screamed this way for so long, I don't think she will stop as long as she lives," but she was mistaken.

I stripped the baby and rubbed her little body with the warm oil and then gave her a few drops of the warm water from a spoon for I felt that her little throat must be parched from her long crying.

She stopped for a moment, the mother sat up in bed and said, "What has happened? Has she gone?" I said, "No, she is just getting quiet." I turned the baby on her little stomach over my knees and gently rubbed her little back. She sobbed and sobbed but soon fell asleep. The door to the kitchen opened softly and the father said, "Is she dead?" I said, "No, she is asleep." He said, "Asleep, woman you have wrought a miracle."

It was no miracle and the baby did not stay asleep only a few minutes at a time until about noon. By that time her naps had quieted her nerves until she slept normally.

Although the baby slept during the greater part of the afternoon the parents were not convinced that she was not ill, and they wanted the doctor to see her. When ever they would call the doctor's wife

Tully with one of her patients. (family photo)

on the telephone she would say, "I must talk to Mrs. Graves for Doctor will want her report on the case."

I told her that so far as I could tell, the baby was all right as she was sleeping quietly but the parents could not feel comfortable until the doctor had seen the baby, as the new mother was as much to be considered as the child, I felt that he should come if possible. He did not get there until about three o'clock in the morning. When he found the baby quiet and all the members of the family asleep, he proceeded to give me a terrible scolding for allowing him to make that long, cold trip out there when he needed to conserve all his strength for the emergency work which he was doing in Philip.

I went home the next afternoon rather disturbed in my own mind. The Downeys felt that I had saved their baby's life and perhaps that of Mrs. Downey also, but I had failed to spare the doctor a long, hard night trip which might be his undoing, and there were hundreds of sick people dependent upon him.

Thank God the flu epidemic finally burned itself out. The war is over and perhaps we can settle down to normal living. I am not sure about that for the war seems to have changed our thinking about things. No one seems to be just the same as they were before the war. We are restless on the farm and I am sure I don't know what to do about help. John does not seem to be able to manage things alone.

Our alfalfa is fine this spring as it will soon be ready for the first cutting. John thought he must have a tarpaulin to cover the stacks while he was building them, for if a rain came up and wet the open stack, it was very likely to heat and burn.

They had no tarpaulins in Philip as large as John wanted and one of the merchants suggested to him that we make one of unbleached muslin and coat it with boiled linseed oil.

John brought home a bolt of muslin and I sewed two widths of it together on the sewing machine. Then we spread it out in the yard and took paint brushes and applied a liberal coating of the oil. When we had it almost covered we ran out of oil. It was late Saturday after-noon and I hated to have John go to town for it would make us so late with the chores. I said, "If I were dampening clothes I would roll them up and let the moisture penetrate the rest of the cloth. I don't see why that would not work with the oil just the same." John readily agreed to try this plan and we rolled the heavy tarpaulin up and carried the roll up near the house hoping that it would be in good condition by morning.

In the middle of the night I was awakened by a strong odor in our room. I said, "John, John, I am sure that I smell smoke!" He said, "Oh, no, it is not smoke that you smell, but the odor of the oil on that tarpaulin." Just then a blaze of light filled the room. I said, "The house is on fire!" We rushed out in our night clothes to find that the tarpaulin had caught fire from spontaneous combustion and that it had set fire to the side of the house.

John jerked the blazing tarpaulin out into the driveway away from the house while I rushed into the kitchen and brought a pail of water and rug. With these I was able to put out the blazing wood on the house in a few moments, but John had more of a struggle with his tarpaulin. When he got it out into the drive away from the shelter of the house the wind blew that burning fragments out into the grass. He was so busy beating this big fire with a wet sack that he could not put out the small fires that were starting. Fortunately for us all, I was able to help him as my fire was out. So that by the time the tarpaulin was a smoldering black mass, I had put out all the little fires and with John surveyed the wreck. I said, "It is all my fault for I told you to roll it up. I did not know that oil would heat and burn like this. Now we will be obliged to go without a tarpaulin during another haying season."

John said, "Never mind the tarpaulin. We should be thankful that our house did not burn. I am sure that I don't see how you were able to put that fire out so quickly in this wind." He forgot that the fire in the house was on the sheltered side and that it had gained but little headway when I got to it.

The rattle snakes have been very bad around our place this year. We have always been bothered with them, but for some reason they seem to be thicker this year than ever. John plowed a fire guard over on Paul's land near the road to help protect some hay land. One night as he was driving some calves home after dark he heard a rattle snake buzz not far from him. He stuck a stick in the sod so that he could find the place, came home and got a lantern and the pitch fork and went back. Sure enough he found that the big rattle snake had crawled under a sod near where he had his stick planted. John was able to dispatch him readily with the pitch fork. He brought home the eleven rattles and a button to show me that he knew rattle snake habits. John has a quart fruit jar almost filled with the rattles from snakes that he has killed since we have been here. I have been trying to get him to destroy them for the Indians say that if the dust from snake rattles gets into your eyes it will cause blindness. I do not know that this is true, but I do not care to try the experiment to find out.

About two weeks ago when John was getting up one morning, he said, "Two of the colts, Nell and Chief, are down in the yard. I wonder how that happens." I said, "Hurry and go down. I just dreamed that Nell was snake bitten." "Your dreaming does not make it so," retorted my husband as he disappeared down the stairs.

In just a moment he called, "Tully, Tully, hurry, hurry! Come and help me! Nell is not bitten badly, but Chief is in terrible shape, I doubt if we can save him!"

He drove the colts into the barn while I stopped in the kitchen long enough to mix a thick paste of soda and vinegar in a bowl. With this in one hand and clean cloths and the kerosene can in the other I went to the barn to help administer our "snake bite" remedies. We always washed the bite with kerosene and then put on a thick coating of the soda and vinegar. By these treatments we have been able to save several of our animals that have been bitten by rattlesnakes. We did not know which one was effective or whether it was the combination that did the work, so we used them all.

Perhaps we were too late in reaching these colts, at any rate as their heads and throats continued to swell rapidly and we were afraid "Chief" would choke to death. John said, "You must get some man to help me. It will be necessary to 'stick' these horses so that some of this poison will drain out."

I got into the car and drove as quickly as I could over to Mr. Downey's. I told him what had happened and that John needed help. He answered my S.O.S. as readily as I had answered his when his wife and baby were sick. He called to his wife that we needed his help for a few hours but he would be back as soon as he could and then we were off.

We could hear "Chief's" labored breathing when we drove up into the yard. John and Mr. Downey used very vigorous measures with him as they cut twenty-one gashes in this face and throat. The poor colt had never known anything but extreme kindness before and he caged about like a wild creature at such treatment.

The men turned him out of the barn and John put a barrel of water near him so that he could put his poor swollen head in the water to cool it for he could not bend his neck to reach into a water hole.

I took Mr. Downey back home. John said when I returned that he had sent to town some neighbor girls for some turpentine to use on the horses. We waited until about noon for these girls to come back. Then they drove leisurely into the yard and said, "We never thought of your turpentine again until we came in sight of your house just now."

John was thoroughly disgusted with their thoughtlessness and he led out a saddle horse and started for town while they were still talking to me. I think he was so excited that he forgot all about the car.

The ride to town and back was good for John's nerves for when he returned said, "You will have to help me now. We must put some of this on "Chief"."

We got the colt into the barn and a fight was staged then and there for the poor beast could not understand why we abused him so terribly. When we finally got him out of the barn he staggered down into Meyers' draw. His breathing seemed more labored than ever. I felt so sorry for the poor animal that I followed him. He had great difficulty with his breathing and went very slowly. I followed and talked quietly to him. At last he stopped under a tree and stood facing me. I talked to him for quite a while, then started back for the house and he followed me. When I got up to the barrel of water that John had fixed for him I put my hand in it and showed him that water was near the top of the barrel. He came up and put his nose in the water. I left him there for I knew that we had done all that we could for him.

The next morning he and Nell were still by the water barrel. Nell was very much better then and Chief is all right now.

We left the barrel filled with water and a few mornings after our experience with the horses John came into the house carrying a baby grouse that he had found in the barrel. It was stiff and wet and cold but still alive. John said, "I thought maybe you would know what to do for this poor thing, it is still alive."

I took it and wrapped it in some warm flannel, let down the oven door and placed the little wild thing there where it would soon get dry and warm. When John came into the house at noon our baby grouse was very much alive. He said, "That is a much larger bird than he looked with his feathers wet. He is old enough to fly." As soon as dinner was over, we took him down and put him in the willow tree where my shrike family had lived for we knew that he was able now to shift for himself.

We have always kept our calves that we feed by hand in a bunch by themselves for we need to put them in the calf barn night and morning to feed them. This year we had twenty-one of them. We have a milking machine now so that we can milk many more cows.

Many people in this country find it necessary to build dams across the draws to store water enough for their stock during the summer for while some of the draws have large water holes on them most of these go dry during the hot summer months.

One of our neighbors, an old man, living about two miles north of us made a large dam across Meyers' draw. Then he stocked his place with Herford cattle and lived very contentedly. His sons used to visit him very frequently from Philip. Sometimes when he was out for a visit he would ride down to our house and often asked John why he did not come up to the dam and shoot ducks.

John said last Wednesday that he was going up to the dam duck shooting, early Thursday morning. Accordingly I fixed him a lunch before I went to bed. The next morning I heard him get up and leave about four o'clock.

I waited with the milking until about seven and then I started the milking machine and milked. I kept working at the chores until I had everything done about ten thirty, but still John failed to come. When he had not come yet at twelve thirty, I started out to see if by any chance he had met with an accident. The car was out of order, and as there was not a horse on the place, I was obliged to walk.

When I reached the dam I called and called for John, but there was no answer. I became much alarmed and hurriedly walked all around the pond, but I could find no trace of him. There was no one at home at the house and no neighbors living near. By this time I was extremely tired and I sat down on the hill side to rest and to think what I should do next. As I was sitting there, I remembered that John had stayed away much longer than he had said he would when he had gone hunting before. Perhaps some other man had come along and wanted him to go and shoot some place else.

As I grew more rested, it seemed the sensible thing for me to do was to go on back home and wait a while longer for surely, if everything was all right, he would not stay away after it was too dark to shoot.

I got home in the late afternoon so very tired after my strenuous day that I layed down on the couch and slept until almost sun down. The milk cows were at the gate when I awoke. I put them in the corral and was on my way up to the house when I saw John coming empty handed. I waited until he came up to me and said, "Tully, I am sorry I stayed so long, for I knew you would be worried, but Mr. Swenson from town came out to the dam. When there was no shooting there, he proposed that we should go to some big water holes up on the North Fork. He had heard that the ducks were coming in there. I went with him, but really I never intended to stay so late as this."

I said, "I know you didn't intend to stay so long John, for after all, 'Man is but a boy grown tall'."

Monday evening when I went for the calves I found one of them dead near a water hole. The next morning another one was dead in the barn. John went right to town for the veterinarian. He said, "Your calves have 'Black Leg'."

We have lost seven of them. There seems to be so many things that are beyond our power to help, to eat up the profits. I feel that I am losing my courage.

The long, hot summer is before us. One man who came out here said, "This is the best next year country that I ever visited. Every one hopes for better things next year." I am no exception to this rule. I am still hoping for better things next year.

Lovingly,
Tully

Life in Rural Community

October 3, 1920

My dear Sara:

When it draws near Thanksgiving time, I always have a homesick feeling around my heart, for our family made much of the holidays, as you well know.

The second or third year that we were in South Dakota, Mrs. Smiley, who lives about ten miles west of Philip on the North Fork of Bad River, invited us to her home for Thanksgiving dinner. She said that as there were six childless couples living near each other who had no relatives in South Dakota with whom they could spend the holiday, she thought that we might enjoy taking turns in entertaining the group on different holidays.

We were delighted with this arrangement and it has been the practice from that time on to spend our holidays together, although not all the families have remained childless, I am happy to say. We have always kept to the original arrangement of taking turns at the entertaining.

Times have been hard and often the gardens did not produce much in the way of vegetables, but these tables fairly groaned with food when the holidays arrived. We have dinner usually in the early afternoon. Sometimes we women folks washed the dishes; but more often we did not for every one of us was anxious to spend the afternoon visiting and singing.

If the house where we were being entertained afforded an instrument, we gathered around that and sang familiar songs until the company had to break up to go home and do the chores, for country folks must be at home at chore time.

It seemed a difficult matter for most of us to get the necessary routine of farm work out of the way in time to go to church on Sunday morning and as it was impossible for us to be away from home in the evening, we were practically cut off from church services.

The ministers from town very kindly offered to come to our school house and hold services for us. We took a basket dinner and planned to serve it about one thirty. We could then get it cleared away and ready for Sunday School and church in time for the minister to get back into town for the evening services.

Sometimes a minister from one church would come and sometimes one from another denomination. It made no difference to us in our community. We always enjoyed a good sermon and we were not particular as to the creed which the minister felt it his duty to expound. We only held these services during the summer months when the days were long for after services were over we would gather in little groups and talk until we were obliged to go home to milk.

I sometimes say that I would not know how to carry on a conversation if I were obliged to talk about anything but cows.

As neither John nor I ever danced we had not attended the dances that were being given at different places through out the community, but when the new home of some very dear friends of

*Philip, 1920. (*First Half Century, Philip, South Dakota*)*

ours, the Olsens, on the North Fork of Bad River, was finished and the neighbors planned a house warming for them, and for entertainment during the evening they were going to dance in the old log house, John and I could not refuse to go.

It seemed, however, that when we wanted to go away from home something always happened to make us late. It was a joke among our friends that we were never on time. This evening was no exception. The calves were no where to be found that night. John hunted in one direction and I in another. I was just coming home about dark when I ran across them bedded down by a shack about a mile from home. They had no intention of coming home. This made us so late with our work that it was almost eleven o'clock before we got started for the party. We thought that we could just cut across the prairie for a few miles and make it much nearer. We were some little distance from home when we started down into a draw. It seemed damp and cold. Then we realized that a very unusual thing had happened, for we had entered a bank of fog.

We wished then that we had stayed in the road for we soon lost our sense of direction and were no long able to be sure just where the water holes were. I had suggested before we left home that we should take the lantern, and once more in our rediculous way of doing things, I was walking ahead carrying the lantern while John drove behind me shouting assurance that I was going in the wrong direction. After some time, we came out upon the highway and the directions were apparent to us both. I climbed back into the buggy and we drove the rest of the way without further trouble. Many of our friends came out to the buggy to greet us, and inquired why we were so late in arriving.

As John helped me down from the buggy he said quietly, "Don't tell them that we were lost; just let on that we were late with our work. We will stay here until daylight."

This was my first all night party. I had often heard that the dances lasted until day break, but I had never hoped to have this experience.

About three o'clock in the morning, I grew so sleepy that I could scarcely keep my eyes open. The whang, whang, of the violins and the monotonous drone of the organ added to my drowsiness. I slipped into the bed room unnoticed and there I found that some mother had made a pallet on the floor and put her two children there to sleep. I snuggled down beside them and covered myself up with my coat and was soon fast asleep.

I didn't sleep long, however, for when I awakened it seem to me that my hip bones had worked through the flesh to the hard floor. I roused myself quickly and went out into the kitchen where I bathed my face in cold water hoping to remove the tell tale traces of sleep.

Once more I joined my friends in the room where they were dancing. I was in hopes that no one had missed me, but such was not the case for as I entered the room I was greeted with "Here you are. We looked everywhere for you. We decided you must have gone off some where and gone to sleep." I was rather non-committal for I simply said, "I don't see why you could think that."

John was tired and cross by the time we had finished the morning chores. He spoke his mind freely about the nonsense of people playing all night who had to work all day.

I heartily agreed with all he had said, but since we had played there was no need to grouch about it so I suggested that we sleep awhile.

When we awakened soon after noon, we were both in a better frame of mind. We talked things over and decided that since we did not dance, that we could find a more suitable time to do our visiting than at all-night parties, and that we would make this our first and last experience of this kind.

One morning very early, just as we were getting up a wagon drove into the yard and a woman's voice called out, "Any body to home?" I called out that I would be down in a moment, yet all the time I was wondering what could have brought any one here at such an early hour. The woman proved to be a neighbor from the north-west. She and her husband with a large family of children had bought a quarter section of land and had moved on it hoping to make a living farming. They had come from the Ozarks and were not too thrifty. Some of the neighbors had tried to persuade them that they had better dig a well, for the water in the waterholes would be unfit for drinking before the hot weather was over. They preferred to wait until necessity made this measure imperative.

When I went out to the wagon to see what my early caller wanted, I found that one of her smaller children was lying on some hay in the back of the wagon. The child was apparently too ill to sit up. The mother said that she had brought her child down to see if I could tell what to do for him, as they were too poor to have a doctor.

I questioned her about his diet and then asked if they were still using the water from the water hole. She answered that they were. We took the child into the house where I made him comfortable on the couch. I put plenty of water on the stove to heat, brought a washtub into the kitchen and then told the mother that it would be necessary for me to go down and help with the milking; but as soon as the water was hot I should like to have her give the child a good hot bath and put on a clean night gown which I had laid out for him, and then I could probably do something for him.

She looked at me for a minute and then said, "Give him a bath? A bath? What is that?" I was thoroughly disgusted with her by this time and I said, "Fill that tub with warm water, then take that soap and wash cloth and scrub his body until it is good and clean. She looked at me incredulously and then said, "What, put water right on his bare hide?"

These two dirty people seemed quite out of keeping with my pretty home. The outside of it was still covered with blue building paper but we had really fixed the inside up until it was homey and comfortable. This too was made possible by my good Seeman friends in Philip.

If you remember, I told you that Mr. Seeman was in the lumber business in Philip. The people were eager to have their houses plastered with plastering that would set quickly, but unfortunately for the lumber people they had a small supply on hand that set too quickly.

One day John was in the lumber yard for some fuel and Mr. Seeman told him about the plastering. He said, "I believe there is enough there to plaster your house and that it will work if you exercise care in handling it. You may take it out with you if you can use it, you are welcome to it. If not, you can throw it in Meyer's draw to help build up your crossing.

Before I came home on Friday night, John had been to see if Mr. Macy, who was a mason, would come and plaster the house for us, and what he would charge for his labor. Mr. Macy was obliged to be away from home a great deal and John had often hauled out fuel and supplies for his family. I think perhaps the Macys felt most grateful to him for hauling out baled hay and storing it in the barn for them. They had been unable to get any hay put up to feed their stock during one winter and accordingly had bought baled hay that been shipped in from east of the Missouri River.

John was not able to get this work done for them before the snows started in the winter. His last few trips were very difficult and since he would not take any pay for the work, Mr. Macy said that he would be very happy to plaster our house for us without charge. I was delighted at the prospect of living once more in a house that was plastered. I could scarcely wait for John to haul the sand so that the work could start.

They tried a small place on the dinning room wall just about dark one evening and early the next morning Mr. Macy came down to see whether this was satisfactory or not so that we would know whether we could use this old plastering or not.

The trial proved satisfactory and the men started to work in earnest that morning. It was interesting to watch the rooms change to the appearance the plastered walls gave them. They seemed to be much smaller after they were plastered but they took on the substantial look of a real house.

When the work was done, and the plastering had thoroughly dried we found that it was very spotted. In some places it was grey and in others it was almost white.

The next winter after the plastering was done John put the casing on the rooms as he could find time. Mr. Seeman came out and helped him several different days. By the time field work started in the spring, this work in the house was finished.

Each of these improvements had made the house much more livable, but still the walls were spotted and ugly.

At Thanksgiving time John and I whitewashed the kitchen; kalsomined the living room a buff color, and papered the dining room a deft blue with a cream ceiling. We finished the woodwork in the kitchen and living room with oak stain and varnish, and the dining room with old English stain. We had an open stairway across one end of the living room. This had been one of my dreams but until now it had been ugly, for it had not had pailings or a rail. Before it was finished I used to think of it as a stairway into a barn loft. Now it was really very good looking with its pailings, rail and treads stained and varnished, and I feel that one more of my dreams has come true.

The plastering and finishing of the inside of the house stands out as one of the big incidents in my life here. All these years there has been that great yearning for a home. After the house was plastered, the outside was still ugly with its blue building paper covering. It was next to impossible to keep this paper in repair for the wind pulled it from under the laths that were supposed to hold it and would play havoc with it before I could rescue it even though I heard it and rushed to save it when it first tore from its fastenings.

One evening I came home from town just about sun down and was putting my horse in the barn, when I saw a man with a satchel strapped under his arm coming from the gate toward the house. He was using a stick for a cane and limping badly so that it was an easy matter for me to get the house some time before he did.

I went to the front door in response to his knock. He greeted me huskily with, "Water, water, I want water." For some reason that I can not explain, I felt this man was an imposter. So that I said as I hooked the screen door, "Very well, I will bring you some water."

I brought a pitcher of water and a glass. He gulped down the first glass full that I poured for him and said, "More," as he handed the glass back to me.

I poured a second glass for him, and as I handed it back to him, I said, "You must have had quite a walk you seem so thirsty. Do you have much farther to go?" He looked at me queerly out of two strange eyes that had a funny glint to them, "Madam, I am not going one foot, no, not one inch farther tonight. I am going to stay right here."

I realized now that I was probably talking to a man who was mentally deranged. John had gone to a neighbors that afternoon for our winter's supply of potatoes. I was not at all sure just when he would return, but I made a bluff by saying, "That will be just as my husband says when he get here. He usually objects very strongly to keeping strangers." At this the man poured out such a volume of abuse at me that I was really frightened. He cursed and swore and called upon the powers above to witness the curses that he was calling down upon my head. He said, "Because I am on foot and poor you turn me from your door. If I were rich and straddle of a broncho you would receive me with open arms."

Just then I heard the roll of a wagon nearing the barn and I knew that John had come and so I said with all the courage that I could command, "We can settle this in a very few minutes. My husband is coming right now. That is his wagon that you can hear."

The man dropped the stick that he had been using for a cane and hurried down across the draw and on over the hill on the other side as fast as he could go. All evidences of his apparent lameness had vanished.

John jumped out of his wagon and came toward the house. I started out to meet him but I shook so badly from fright that I could scarcely walk.

John came up to me and said, "Who is that man? What did he want?"

I just stood before him dumb with the tears streaming down my face.

John rushed past me into the house and came out with his gun. I said, "Don't John!" He said, "If that man harmed you I'll kill him!"

Prairie fires were a great menace to pioneer life.
(Haaken Horizons)

I said, "He did not harm me; he just frightened me by swearing and cursing so terribly. Besides I think he is insane."

There really was nothing to be done about the matter excepting to let the man go on his way. His visit left me more afraid to stay alone for fear of people, but I was in constant dread of prairie fires. They were not uncommon, but still there was no need of frenzied fear for in all the years that we lived on the farm, only four fires came very near us. Yet fires are the greatest menace to pioneer life.

One Sunday afternoon an automobile load of men stopped at our house for some drinking water. They had only gone a short distance on their way out when they had some car trouble and were delayed for sometime. Just as their car pulled away we saw the fire start in the draw where they had been stalled. We each took a pail of water and a jute sack and ran to an old road that was in the path of the fire. The fire was there almost as soon as we were. The grass was short here and we were able to put the fire out before it crossed the road. Not much damage was done, but it showed how quickly these prairie fires could travel.

In Hay Draw the grass grew much more luxuriantly than it did around our place. The farmers in that section used to plow several furrows all around their places as these made good fire guards. Unless the wind was blowing very hard, the fire could usually be beaten out at these guards. In case of a high wind the Russian thistles, which grew very prolifically in the patches of plowed land that the homesteaders have left behind them as mute evidence of blasted hopes, roll ahead of the fire and start it afresh in places where it has been extinguished.

The men also used the roads and fire guard to back fire from, for a fire must burn itself out if it has no fuel to feed upon.

The men in this township have bought a large tarpaulin which they dip in a water hole and then fasten one end of it to the horn of a saddle. Dragging this wet tarpaulin over the dry grass moistens it enough so that it gives the men an opportunity to put the fire out here. In early days the cow boys used to kill a beef and drag a quarter of it with their saddle horses in this same way.

It is an unwritten law in this country that when any person sees the smoke of a prairie fire, that he goes immediately and helps to put it out. This might seem the logical thing to do, but it is not always an easy thing to do, for in a cattle country there are many annoying things that happen in neighborhoods that lead to hard feelings, and neighborhood quarrels. This feeling sometimes becomes so intense that the quarrels are carried into the courts.

It is not easy for one man to go to the help of a neighbor if that neighbor happens to be his bitter enemy.

Hay Draw had a number of families that were not on speaking terms but one day when some passing motorist started a prairie fire in this community by tossing a burning cigarette into the dry grass by the roadside, every able bodied man and woman rushed out to help fight the fire.

The wind was blowing and much valuable hay land was soon burned over while the fire was sweeping on in the direction of stacks of hay and farm buildings which lay in its path. The fire burned so rapidly that the water holes were too far away to be of any real service. Then the men loaded barrels into wagons, the women would go to the wells, or water holes, and fill these barrels with water and haul them back to the men who were on the fire line.

All neighbor hood quarrels were forgotten, for all these people were faced with a common danger. Sometimes the women who were hauling water together had not spoken to each other for a matter of months or years.

Late afternoon saw the fire under control and most of the fighters found themselves several miles from home. With the friendliness which the afternoon's fighting had established among those people, one woman who was about ready to start for home gathered up all her neighbors into her wagon and they started off.

They had only gone a short distance when each person began to become conscious of the presence of some of his former enemies. The danger past, but they still had several miles to go before any of them reached home and as no two of them were friends the conversation lagged. Can you imagine such a thing as this to happen in a wagon load of women, for there was only one man in the crowd. His problem now proved to be greater than that of any of the women for as he looked down the road ahead of him he recognized his lawyer's car. He could not face the ordeal of allowing this man to see him riding in the same wagon with all those unfriendly women. To escape being seen he crawled into one of the empty water barrels and rode the rest of the way home.

The other prairie fire occurred in the winter time. I was teaching in the little country school. The ground was covered with patches of snow so that the thought of prairie fire had not entered my mind. One morning I saw a big cloud of smoke to the south west of the school house and I became concerned immediately for a strong wind was blowing from that direction. I had the school children put on their wraps and pile their books upon their desks. I told them that we would wait until the fire came upon us. When it had passed by we would go out on the burned ground where we would be safe. The Russian thistles had grown so thickly in the banking around the school house that it seemed quite probable that if the fire reached the school house at all that there would be no way of saving it for there was no water near enough to be of any great help.

The children were very sensible about it. We sang songs and repeated poetry. Soon one of the father's rode up on horseback to tell us to do just as we had planned to do in case the fire came to the school house. He told us not to be afraid that there would be plenty of men there to help us in case we needed help. Our fears were groundless for the men were able to keep the fire from spreading far in our direction, although it did burn over several miles before they were able to get it under control.

This fire started in a peculiar manner. There was a cripple man who had spent the night with relatives in the community. He drove a team and buggy. After he was once in his buggy he could go about over the country as he chose.

On this particular morning he did not light his pipe until he was in his buggy and well started on his day's trip. He said that he soon smelled burning wool. He thought that some of the burning tobacco had fallen from his pipe onto his clothing, but upon investigation he found that his buggy robes were on fire and he threw them out of the buggy, then he discovered that his clothing and his buggy was also on fire. He got out of the buggy as quickly as his crippled condition would allow him to do so, but this was not in time to keep the burning robes from blowing into the grass by the road side and setting it on fire. This frightened the horses and they ran away dragging the burning buggy after them. This set fire to the prairie as far as they went. They were able to free themselves from the buggy so that neither of them were burned.

The crippled man rolled about in the snow until he extinguished the fire from his clothing so that no real damage was done, save to burn over some good pasture land.

One of the men was kind enough to ride past the school house on his way home and tell us all the details about the fire, and also to assure us that we were no longer in any danger as the fire was completely out.

The people here are so extremely kind to me, Sara. This life is hard, and the repeated disappointments and failures in the farming venture would make it impossible for me to live here if it were not for these true friends of mine. I miss my family tremendously, but in a way my friends satisfy the longing I feel for you. I hope you will not misunderstand this statement.

Sister Anne writes me that she has a second daughter. I do not envy her for I know that she is a wonderful mother. She used to tell me in her letters after she finished Normal school and went to teaching that she felt that she would make kindergarten teaching her life work for she enjoyed it so tremendously. Now she writes that she knows no woman could be happier than she is with her home and her family. She says that she will never come back to her homestead to live but that she has so much sentiment about it that she does not want to sell it.

June and Paul sold their land for $2500.00. They have a new home in Fairbury, Nebraska. Paul is making money there.

Since mother is in Wakefield, you know more about her than I do. Write often, please, and tell me much about her.

Lovingly,
Tully

On, On into the Sunset

My dear Sara:

Several years have elapsed since I wrote to you last. I have not had the heart to write to you as I used to in earlier years when life was before me and the failures of a few years seemed such a small part of life itself.

Perhaps it is because of my unhealthy thinking. I do not know what else could cause one loss after another in such quick succession. "Troubles never come single handed," seems meant for me for I have scarcely been able to raise my head up and get my bearings after one misfortune until I would be over taken with another.

The last year seemed the most hectic of any that we had spent here. I can not even yet write to you the details of that winter. At any rate, we lost half of our herd of cattle with "Hemorragic Sceptecimia" whatever that is. After the first cow died we sent at once for vaccine and had the entire herd vaccinated. While our loss was more than we were able to stand, financially, we were glad that we were able to save half of them.

This loss completely broke my spirit. It seemed like a hopeless thing to struggle for years at frightful odds to get a start and then to have it swept away in such a short time, almost over night.

John was wedded to the farm and he clung to it with dogged determination in spite of all the years of failure that we had been through. Knowing his feeling about the farm, I was much surprised one day when he came home from town and said that he had a job down there.

We were able to rent the farm to a young man who had gone to school to me when he was a boy. As he and his wife were both strong and liked to live in the country, it seemed that this might be a good solution of our problem.

I had been elected to teach in Philip again for the next year. This made me very happy for so much fencing had been done between our house and the country school house that it was necessary for me to open seven barbed wire gates on my way to my rural school. This was quite out of the question when the weather was below zero.

We held an auction sale and sold off our cattle, horses, farm machinery and any other things that we did not care to move into town; but I kept all my pretty things that I knew I would want when we established a home in Philip.

The strain of over work had almost wrecked Miss Lee's health, so that she sold her share in the hotel partnership to her partner, Miss Owen, and located in Sioux City where she could receive better medical attention and be among her old friends.

Miss Owen rented the dining room of the hotel to a man who did not care to rent all of the hotel. She kept the part of the hotel used for lodging which she planned to rent to make her living. She reserved a suite of rooms in the front part of the hotel on the second floor where she planned to live. She invited John and me to share this suite with her and she provided a place in the basement for us where I could do our cooking. This seemed a pleasant arrangement and we had made several trips to the farm to bring in my personal treasure so that our new living quarters would take on a more home like appearance.

We had been living here only a few weeks when one morning about two o'clock we were awakened by the sound of the fire bell. We looked out of the window and saw that the fire was in the furniture store just across the street from the hotel. John was dressed and gone in less time than it takes to tell about it. I stopped long enough to empty the contents of the dresser drawers into one of the bed sheets; then I took the other one and wrapped our clothing in this. I went into Miss Owen's room to see if she needed me. I found her beside herself with the excitement of it all. I asked her if she had called the guests. As she had not done so, I hurriedly went down the halls and roused the people. Some of them rushed out into the halls in scanty attire to ask if they would have time to dress before leaving the hotel.

There were no lights anywhere in the building. By the time I reached the bed room that led out from the parlor the building was filled with smoke and I could hear the men shouting that the hotel was on fire.

The woman in the parlor bed room called to me to come and help her for she had become so confused that she could not find her way out of the room. I led her into the back hall where she could see her way out and rushed back upstairs to be sure that all the people had left their rooms. When I came to room twenty-eight, I found the door locked and no amount of knocking would bring any response from the sleeper inside. In sheer desperation, I finally kicked on the door until a sleepy voice said, "What do you want?" I told him that the hotel was on fire and that he would have to hurry if he escaped.

I rushed back up to our room to get the bundles of things that I had left on the beds but I found the room in flames so that it was impossible for me to get into it.

The part of the hotel where we were was built of cement blocks so that I had felt that it would not burn. It did burn, however, and burned very quickly. Those who watched the fire from the street said that the hotel was burning in ten minutes after the first alarm was sounded.

The furniture store was a frame structure that burned like tinder. As soon as the front windows of that store broke with the heat, the fire leaped across the street and caught the awnings all along the front of the hotel. In just an instant, the glass in the front windows broke from this heat together with that of the fire from across the street, the rooms were soon in flames.

I made my way downstairs through the smoke to the office where I took the hotel books, register and what cash was in the cash drawer and groped my way down the smoke filled back hall to the outdoors.

By this time the buildings on both sides of the street were burning. The volunteer fire fighters were putting up a brave fight, but the frame buildings burned like card board boxes. The high wind carried the flames quickly from one building to another.

It looked for a time as though even the residential section of town would burn, but the heroic efforts of the fire men confined the fire to two blocks of business houses on the main street. This practically wiped out the business section of our little town of Philip that

*Philip after the fire. (*Haaken Horizons*)*

we all loved so dearly. These brave people were crushed by this frightful blow but their spirit was not broken and they immediately started to rebuild as soon as the ruins stopped smoldering so that they could be cleared away.

It seems that I should not mention our loss when you think of what my friends had suffered, yet to us, our clothing and personal effects were about all that we had left as we had lost everything else at the sale. Once more it was necessary to face life with nothing.

Mrs. Newcomb, who had a new home well out of the fire zone, offered to rent us a room in her house. We lived here for several months until she sold it.

We moved again, this time into two rooms. The third move found us living in the Seeman house. They had long since gone back to Des Moines.

My school work in Philip was as interesting as ever, but I began to long for some larger field where there would be some chance of promotion or progress in my profession.

I had not attended summer school for a long time, and as I felt the need of brushing up on methods and getting some new ideas about my work, I decided to go to the Spearfish Normal to summer school. While I was in Spearfish, I learned of a vacancy in the upper grades at Salt Creek, Wyoming. This made a strong appeal to me, and I immediately applied for the position; not only because it carried about a five hundred dollar a year increase in salary, but it seemed to me that as it was necessary for John and me to start over, that it would be better to get into some place where there would be a greater number of jobs for him to choose from. Sure he could find some work that he would enjoy doing in an oil field.

I was most delighted when I was elected to teach at Salt Creek. I had written to John very fully about my plans and I expected to find him very enthusiastic about them. John's letters about my new position in Salt Creek were rather indefinite. He did not show much enthusiasm and yet he had not said that he would not go with me.

Then summer session was over and I caught the first train out, which reached Philip about midnight, and sure enough John was at the station to meet me. As soon as I looked into his eyes I knew that he had good news for me.

He evidently had intended to save his surprise until we reached home but as we walked along the deserted streets the clump, clump, clump of our steps, seemingly loud enough to awaken the sleeping villagers, we did not talk until John stopped suddenly and said, "I can't wait any longer to tell you that at last we have won, for our south field yielded a big crop of flax seed and now the alfalfa field is loaded with seed."

This seed would probably bring from six to ten dollars a bushel on the market and that would mean that our years of hard work had not been in vain.

I was too astonished to think intelligently. All I could say was, "Can this be true? Can this be true?" By this time we had reached our home and as we sat down to talk the situation over I said, "John, why didn't you tell me this sooner? I have resigned my position here and have signed my contract in Salt Creek. What shall I do?" John said, "Yes. You wrote me that you were going to do that and I have no objections whatever for you will probably never be happy on the farm again. This good crop has given us a chance to sell the farm. You go on to Salt Creek as you have planned and find a job for me there. I will stay here and sell the crop and close up the deal on the farm sale and come on later."

During this talk with John the feeling of loss and failure seemed to leave me and I realized for the first time in years that we had not lost. While our venture in farming had not brought financial returns, it had brought spiritual values which only come to people who live through hardship without becoming embittered.

Of course it was right for us to move on for the first generation of pioneers breaks the soil and endures the hardships that are unavoidable in every virgin country.

The following generation reaps the benefits of all this hard labor and suffering and carry on to success. We had not failed, we had won for our work was done. It was time for us to move on and let the younger generation start where we had left off.

So it was arranged that I should go into the new field and he would stay behind until such a time as I would be able to find a job for him.

My friends begged me not to leave Philip, but it seemed to me that perhaps I was being shown a way out. Many of my friends came to the station to see me off and as I stood on the back platform of the car waving good bye to them, it seemed that leaving this group of faithful friends was one of the hardest things that I had ever been called upon to do.

I realized that I was going into a new field to undertake new work, to meet new people, make new friends, and perhaps we would establish our new home out here in this place that was new to me.

The train rounded the curve and my friends were cut off from my sight. As I turned to go back into the coach, I stopped suddenly and looked, for there before me, the setting sun was just at the horizon, sending its long streaks of light far up into the sky, painting the clouds the most vivid red and orange. I watched until the sun sank and brilliant coloring gave way to the purples, blues and grays.

Then I went into the coach and sat down realizing more fully than ever before that I knew I was going all along, somewhere out west, "On, on into the sunset."

Lovingly,
Tully

Afterword

In 1926 Estella moved to California, where she worked as house-mother in the girl's dormitory at Humboldt State University. Subsequently she obtained a B.A. degree and became the rural supervisor in Kings, Tuolumne, and Fresno counties. In this capacity she developed and successfully applied new theories in the field of rural education and speech correction in children. The experience she gained enabled her to obtain a Master's Degree at Stanford University in 1930.

That same year, having previously been divorced from Orley Culp, Estella married J. Harl Tener, assistant superintendent of Kern County schools. Orley Culp remained on the land in Haakon County, South Dakota, until 1926 and passed away in Philip on May 3, 1935. The Teners moved to Wasco, California, in 1939, where Estella spent her final years suffering from blindness. She succumbed to a long illness in January of 1949.

Further Reading

Elsie Hey Baye, ed. *Haakon Horizons*. Philip, South Dakota: State Publishing, 1982.

Philip L. Gerber, ed. Bachelor Bess: *The Homesteading Letters of Elizabeth Corey, 1909–1919*. Iowa City: University of Iowa, 1990.

Linda Hasselstrom. *Roadside History of South Dakota*. Missoula, Montana: Mountain Press Publishing Company, 1994.

First Half Century, Philip, South Dakota. Pioneer Publishing House, 1957.